D1034894

Eyewitnesses at the Cross

This is for Bettie, who transforms my days into joys,
for Bill, Carolyn, Dick, Eileen, Francis, Helen,
Jean, Joe, Larry, Leo, Libby, Madelyn, Vic
and Wally, of Delmar Baptist Church in St. Louis;
Anita, Caroline, Clarence, Dan, Donna, Ed,
Jack, Jan, Jim, Joanne, John, Ken and Shirley
of Calvary Baptist Church in Denver, who
translated my ideas into flesh, and
for Karen, who transcribes my scrawl into script.

Contents

Preface

The weeks preceding Easter can be the occasion for profound worship. It is a time when Christian people seem uniquely susceptible to deeply moving religious experiences. For that reason it behooves the preacher to give special attention to the seven Sundays culminating in Easter. Those may be weeks of sermonic enrichment for the minister and worship excitement for the people.

A few years ago my thinking was stimulated by an article in the *Christian Century.* It was entitled "Worship in an Age of Immediacy" and discussed what it referred to as the crisis in worship. It said, "The word-package that constitutes most of Protestant worship just isn't turned on for a generation accustomed to participation and involvement."[1] One observation in this article struck me as being indisputably true. The author said that an older person who misses a worship service is likely to ask, "What did he say?" However, a younger person is more apt to ask, "What happened?" Our services are word-packages. The preacher has lots and lots to say, but too little happens! Worship, I believe, must become the scene of action—a place/time where something more than the making, speaking, and hearing of words occurs.

[1] James F. White, "Worship in an Age of Immediacy," *Christian Century,* vol. 85, no. 8 (February 21,1968), p. 228.

9

This book is offered in response to the call for the improvement of worship. It contains the modest experimentation in which two congregations have participated during the Lenten season. Although the whole structure of the worship hour needs to be the subject of much study and effort, the material in this book is designed for use during the sermon time. Too often creativity is identified with radical departures from traditional services. It is possible to be creative and innovative within the traditional structures. Many sanctuaries present nearly insurmountable obstacles to redesigning worship as a happening. Many churches have orders of service that are as sacred and immutable as the Decalogue. However, the sermon time is the minister's own time. Within those twenty to twenty-five minutes, most congregations will grant the preacher the freedom to exercise as much creativity as he can muster. If the experience of this preacher is any indication, they will more than grant it—they will encourage and applaud it.

It is obvious to the reader that this book is a word-package. Admittedly the materials in this volume are sets of words packaged in a slightly variant manner. Yet, in services where these materials were used, something different did happen. Worshipers departed talking about not only what they had heard from the preacher but also what had happened in the hour. They returned on subsequent Sundays with a measure of reverent expectancy, wondering what surprise was in store for them or what biblical character they were going to meet. The dramatic content was minimal, to be sure, but even it was considerably more than most Protestant worship had contained.

The use of these materials requires the participation of lay people. It has been a source of delight to me to witness the eagerness with which lay people share this way in worship. Frequently they are asked to take up the offering, or make a stewardship appeal, or imitate a preacher on laymen's or women's Sundays. Seldom are they asked to share in the proclamation of the gospel. In at least two congregations there have been people waiting to do this "preaching." These materials provide for the active involvement of one lay person each week. However, the worshiping lay people tend to identify with this one of their number and thus their sense of participation in the worship is enhanced. Other lay persons may become involved through the management of the simple staging requirements or the coaching of dramatic skills.

These materials are provided as usable resources. I hope they will encourage other preachers to express their own creativity and to seek ways of making worship happen for the people in the pews.

LaRue A. Loughhead

Part One
Inside Story

Introduction

The story of our Lord's Passion contains many characters. The names of a large number of them are well known because they played major roles in the drama. The gospel record has made them famous or infamous. However, there are some minor characters whose roles in the Passion drama are barely mentioned or merely implied. We assume that these lesser lights had their own stories to tell. Their participation in the drama may not have affected the sequence of events or changed the ultimate outcome. Yet their feelings and reactions might very well shed light on the meaning of it all.

On the pages that follow, seven of these minor characters tell their "inside stories." The names of two of them are familiar— Simon of Cyrene and Joseph of Arimathea. The name of another is a matter of historical fact—Claudia Procula, wife of Pilate. The others are fictional names assigned by a reverent imagination. Although some of these individuals are not actually mentioned in the New Testament, the assumption of their existence is not without justification. Someone owned the Garden of Gethsemane and the Palm Sunday donkey. A nameless maid was there to recognize Peter in the courtyard, and a nameless Pharisee had that coin of Caesar's. Care has been exercised not to do violence to either the spirit or the facts of the gospel accounts. The intent is to

13

amplify and enrich those accounts rather than challenge or confuse them.

The same plan is followed in the telling of each of the inside stories. First, a passage of Scripture is suggested for reading which either mentions or implies the character to be heard. Second, the character tells his story in a first person monologue. Third, the preacher responds to the story, making it relevant to the life of the people in the pew.

The impact of this sermonizing can be increased by careful attention to elemental mechanics. The lay person who is to give the monologue should be chosen with great care. The ideal would be for this person to be costumed appropriately in biblical garb and to relate the entire story from memory. The length of the monologue makes that highly improbable. An alternative is to have the person read from a unique location in the chancel and wear a robe of a contrasting color to that of the preacher and choir. Robes can be secured at low cost from rental companies and a large variety of colors is available. The person should be exceedingly familiar with the material and should spend considerable time in practice on location. Adequate sound projection is an absolute necessity. There is nothing more frustrating than being unable to hear. A person who has had some experience in dramatics should be asked to help coach the characters. If focusing additional light on the character is possible, that will emphasize his message.

Although these materials are designed to add action to worship, unnecessary movement and mechanics should be kept to a minimum. The probability of congregational acceptance is increased when the chancel or platform furniture is not displaced or relocated. It would be better not to have additional lighting than have it placed in a way that is distracting to the people and appears to convert the chancel into a stage. Further, as the focus shifts from preacher to character and back to preacher, movement should be minimal and natural. It is important that the preacher and the character spend time together. Every phrase and action of the sermonizing should be planned and rehearsed. The best of material can be subverted by the simplest human or mechanical flaw.

It would be a happy by-product if this layman/preacher proclamation issued in a new and deepened relationship between the two and generated a fresh interest in the study of the biblical passages which inspired the presentation.

14

1. Nathan: Pharisee with a Problem

Scripture: Matthew 22:15-22

NATHAN SPEAKS

It was late when I got home. Rebecca and the children were asleep. I didn't mind. It had been a long, tense meeting and I was glad not to have to talk about it. As quietly as possible I got ready for bed and slipped beneath the covers. Rebecca stirred and mumbled, "Nathan, is that you?" I was tempted to say, "Who else would it be?" Instead I said simply, "Yes, dear." She added, "It must be awfully late. I don't see how you men find so much to talk about." And then she was asleep again. How little she knew! We had had plenty to talk about! Trouble was brewing and no one was certain yet what would happen. I lay on my back, cupped my hands beneath my head, stared at the rough ceiling, and pondered what I had agreed to do.

You see, I'm a Pharisee and proud to be one. The word "Pharisee" means separated, and we try to be separated—separated from the unclean and defiling things around us. We pride ourselves on not compromising in any way. We want to be as true and pure as possible. Not everyone agrees with us on how to be faithful Jews here in occupied Jerusalem. As a matter of fact there are strong differences of opinion among us.

The Sadducees, bless their priestly souls, are so—well, they're so priestly. They scurry about the temple, hover around the altar

15

making sure that everything is precisely the way it ought to be. If the written law says something should be so many inches wide and so many inches long, that's the way it must be and the Sadducees will make very sure of it. Don't misunderstand me. I love the temple. I'm there every time the great doors swing open. But the Sadducees are so wrapped up in it they forget other things. I've heard it said they would even bargain with the Romans if it would guarantee their temple wouldn't be harmed.

If the Sadducees would deal with the Romans to save the precious temple, there are others who would risk their lives to kill those same Romans. Yes, we've got our share of radicals. They hate the very sight of the enemy. Let a Roman tunic walk by and they seethe with rage. "Zealots" they're called, and they despise anyone who compromises with the Romans. As they see it, the only way to set things right in Palestine is to run the enemy out. They're just waiting for the right leader to come along—a leader who will mobilize public sentiment and sound a call to arms. Then Israel will be liberated by force.

We Pharisees are a different sort. We want no traffic with the Romans, but we want none of the violence of the Zealots either. We try to be good, law-abiding Jews. We think the best way for us to remain alive and distinct is to keep our faith and customs as pure as possible. It's not easy. There are hundreds of laws and regulations we've developed over the years. They regulate almost everything we do. We believe those laws are of God. We obey them because we're convinced Jehovah wants us to and we're convinced obeying them will keep us together as a people.

So, I lay there that night, sleepless. I thought about how Rebecca and I tried so hard to be good Jews, how carefully we avoided any compromise or weakening of our standards. And I thought about this latest threat. The special meeting had been called because of it. The matter we discussed so long was what to do about a man named Jesus. Apparently he'd been going around the countryside openly challenging some of our cherished laws and customs. He was now in Jerusalem. The Sadducees were mad because he disrupted their business at the temple one day. The Zealots weren't quite sure where he stood. Things he reportedly said sounded like insurrection; yet he appeared peaceful. All of us at the meeting agreed he was a threat. If people took him seriously, much we Pharisees held dear would soon disappear. On and on we talked.

16

What could we do? Was there anything we could do? Would he upset the Romans? Should we simply let him alone? Finally we decided to attempt to find out what his position was. We agreed that a few of us should try to get some answers from him. Unfortunately, I was chosen to be among his questioners. It was dreading this assignment which robbed me of sleep most of the night.

The next morning came much too early. I would have preferred to stay in bed. However, those of us who had been chosen had arranged to meet and work out our plan. So, I got up, did the usual things—ate, prayed, and such—said good-bye to Rebecca and was on my way. The others had gathered near the temple wall. There was quite a crowd nearby. In the midst of the crowd was our threat himself, the much talked-about Jesus. We weren't the only ones who were interested in him. A few Sadducees were on hand, and I recognized a Zealot here and there. The situation was made to order. We Pharisees quickly conferred on tactics. One had a brilliant idea. He proposed to ask Jesus about the tribute money. The Romans required each Jew to pay tribute to Caesar. There were special coins made for this purpose. We hated those coins because they had Caesar's image on them. It was against our principles to have images of any human being, let alone one like Caesar, who claimed to be divine. We decided to ask Jesus if Jews should pay the tribute money. It seemed like a stroke of genius: If he said "No"—then he would be guilty of insurrection and would be arrested immediately. If he said "Yes"—then he would lose the masses who resented being told to support Rome. So we edged our way into the crowd and waited for the right time to put our question. It came and one of my friends spoke up, "Tell us, Jesus, should a Jew pay tribute money to Caesar?" Jesus looked at us standing there. I guess it was obvious we were together. After thinking a moment, he held out his hand and said, "Do you have a coin I could examine?" Hurriedly I reached beneath my sash for the bag of coins. I opened it, poured out the contents, and selected one of Caesar's coins. I placed it in his hand. He turned the coin over, looked at it, and then smiled a knowing smile. "Whose image is this here on the coin?" "Caesar's," I said. "Oh," said Jesus, "you've already got one of Caesar's coins. Hmmm? I don't know what you're doing with Caesar's money, but if I were you, I would give back to Caesar what belongs to him." Then, after pausing, he

17

went on, "And I would give to God what belongs to Him." So there I was! I was the one who got caught, not Jesus. We still didn't know where Jesus stood, but everyone knew where I stood. I had Caesar's money in my purse. Yet what else could I have done? As a good Jew I despised the image of Caesar as much as anyone. But, if I had refused to pay the tax, I would have been thrown into prison. Rebecca and the children would have suffered for my convictions. Pharisee that I am, loyal Jew that I am, I still have to be realistic.

THE PREACHER REFLECTS

Nathan was caught all right—caught in compromise. He has our sympathies in that. We don't sympathize with his attitude toward Jesus. We do sympathize with his dilemma about Caesar and the taxes. Nathan, typical of the Pharisees of his day, was a good man of unquestioned integrity and unimpeachable character. Further, he was a good Jew of firm conviction and solid beliefs. Like other Pharisees he was concerned about the erosion of the faith. Many did not take the faith as seriously as they once did. Many were careless and casual in their observance of the age-old customs. Many were adopting the ways of the world. Nathan's answer was to stand firm and uncompromising. Yet the simple realities of his life involved him in a compromising situation.

Ah, but you say, "Nathan was not real. You've made him up." That's true. He is not specified or named in the New Testament and lacks reality in that sense. But he is most real in another sense. Every Jew, any Jew, living in that day and that land occupied by a hostile power, had to make an accommodation to the real world. Circumstances plainly were not ideal for being Jewish. So Nathan, hating compromise, compromised.

And what of us? Are circumstances ideal for being Christian? Is there a slow or not so slow erosion of the faith taking place? In our day, is it necessary for the Christian who takes his faith seriously to make a less than ideal accommodation to an essentially non-Christian world? Let's think about that! Let's think about it against the background of this Caesar and God business. "Render . . . to Caesar the things that are Caesar's, and to God the things that are God's."

CAESAR IS REAL

Caesar is real, isn't he? He is real and that makes compromise

18

necessary. Caesar was real to Nathan and to Jesus. He was ever present in the Roman soldier, ever felt in the rules and regulations, taxes, and such. He was real, and if a Jew wanted to stay alive or out of prison, he had to compromise. He had to accommodate his faith to the hostile environment. Caesar is no less real to us. We are living with an illusion if we think this is a Christian world or even a Christian nation. It is a simple fact that many of the presuppositions, goals, and standards of our society are in direct opposition to our avowed faith. Caesar is real in our hedonistic, hell-bent-for-pleasure society; in our materialistic, "thingafication" of all life; in our super patriotism that admits no error; in our ghettoized, racist-ridden cities and suburbs. Caesar is real, and if the Christian wants to remain a part of this society, he has to compromise. He must accommodate his faith to this hostile environment. Caesar is real and that makes compromise necessary, as necessary for us as for Nathan.

That word "compromise" has been a dirty word in certain Christian circles. I'm not proposing that we baptize it now. However, I am suggesting that the art of being a Christian in this day and in this land is the art of compromise. In a society that is not totally Christian, the individual Christian must decide where and to what extent he can operate on Christian principles. Let's take an example: love is a Christian absolute. We are to love everybody, everyone at all times. We are to love the deserving or undeserving, the lovely and unlovely. Society does not operate on that absolute. The Christian's task is to take that absolute of love and locate those places in his life and society where he can apply it at least in modest measure. It is thus the Christian's task to relativize the absolute. Don't be frightened by those words—listen to them: It is the Christian's task to relativize the absolute.[1] It is his task to take the absolutes and make them applicable wherever he can, to whatever degree he can, in this less than ideal world. That is the art of compromise as practiced by the Christian. Compromise is not undertaken to weaken an absolute, but a compromise is made to implement that absolute if only imperfectly. We compromise, not to get rid of an absolute, but to get hold of as much of an absolute as possible. Obviously then, the crucial matter is the why of compromise. The Christian compromises not to weaken the

[1] Joseph Fletcher uses this phrase "relativize the absolute" in his book *Situation Ethics* (Philadelphia: The Westminster Press, 1966), p. 45.

19

faith in order for it to be more acceptable in an evil society. He compromises to give at least partial expression to his faith with the hope that this evil world will become increasingly acceptable to God. So the Christian engages in calculating compromise. He figures the angles, calculates all the possibilities, then pushes love in there, infiltrates brotherhood in here. He does that not to weaken the faith, but to express it if only in approximation. If Caesar were not real, if the kingdom of God had arrived fully, it might be otherwise. But Caesar is real and that makes compromise necessary.

GOD IS GOD

On the other hand, God is God, and that makes compromise unthinkable. It may sound like double-talk to say with one breath that compromise is necessary and with the next that compromise is unthinkable. This contradiction is expressed to stress that there are places where the Christian must compromise and places where he must not. Going back to Nathan for a moment, it appears that Jesus did not object strenuously to the payment of the tribute money to Caesar. No such objection was mentioned. It was Caesar's coin. He made it, so Jesus advised giving it back to him. "Render . . . to Caesar the things that are Caesar's." "But," said he, "don't render unto Caesar what is God's. Render unto God what is God's, and when you've given God his due, there isn't much of value left for Caesar." God is God and there are things that ought to be rendered unto him that should never be rendered unto Caesar. Caesar is real, yes—and that makes compromise necessary. But God is God, and that makes some compromise unthinkable.

To God and God alone is due worship, ultimate allegiance, complete trust, final obedience. If Caesar wants any of these, he shall not have them. They belong to God as God—to God only— and compromise there is unthinkable. Throughout all time, Christians have had to make accommodations to unchristian environments. They have accepted Caesar as real and have worked out their compromises, implementing and spreading the faith as best they could. But whenever Caesar has decided he is Lord, there has been no compromise. Christians have gone to prison, been burned at stakes, thrown into concentration camps, suffered untold indignities. God is God and no other.

In another context, one preacher has said that God insists on

20

being Project 1.[2] He will not be Project 2 or Project 3. He insists on being God—Project 1. And as God, there are things that are his due that ought to be given to no other. A minister from Ohio wrote of a rebellion he had on his hands one year on the Sunday nearest July 4. (I cite this not as the summation of what I've said, but as a single illustration.) It was the custom in that church worship service to remain seated during the singing of the second hymn. On this particular Sunday, the second hymn was "America the Beautiful," and they sang it while seated. The congregation was in a turmoil. How could the preacher have been so irreverent as to remain seated and encourage them to remain seated while singing about America? Writes the preacher, "It's perfectly all right apparently, to sit down for 'O God, Our Help in Ages Past' but irreverent to do so when we sing about our nation."[3] No one raised a voice against any irreverence shown God. Who was Project 1 that morning in that congregation?

Caesar is real, but Caesar is not God. God is God. Worship, ultimate allegiance, complete trust, final obedience are his due, not Caesar's. Compromise there is unthinkable. Caesar is real—that makes compromise necessary. God is God—that makes compromise unthinkable.

Nathan's coin had the image of Caesar on it. Caesar had it made that way. His image on it meant that it belonged to him. "Then God said, 'Let us make man in our image . . .'" (Genesis 1:26). Man has been made with the image of God on him or in him. God made us that way. His image in us means that we belong to him and ought to give ourselves back to him.

[2] Charles B. Templeton, *Life Looks Up* (New York: Harper & Row, Publishers, 1955), p. 180.

[3] Cornelius Loew, *Modern Rivals to Christian Faith*, Layman's Theological Library (Philadelphia: The Westminster Press, 1966), p. 43.

21

2. Benjamin: Businessman with a Garden

Scripture: Mark 14:26, 32-50

BENJAMIN SPEAKS

I'm not a religious man. My friends might be surprised to hear me say that, but I think it's true. Oh, I do the usual things. Sarah and I have kept the Sabbath since the day we were married. When the children came along, we made the customary offerings at the temple. As they grew up, we saw to it they were properly instructed by the rabbis. The holy days always are happy days in our home. Whenever Caiaphas and the other priests decide renovation is needed at the temple, public-spirited Benjamin makes a substantial contribution. It still thrills me every time I enter the temple or catch sight of its towers gleaming in the sun. Yet I don't think of myself as a religious man.

To be honest with you, I'm a busy man. Like my father before me, I'm a businessman here in Jerusalem. I'm in trade and commerce and that's a busy life. Jehovah has been good to me. Things haven't always been easy and they're not very easy right now. The Romans are always breathing down our necks, watching everything we do, checking to make sure we don't cheat them out of a single tax shekel. But with all the ups and downs, I've done quite well. I don't mean that I'm a leading citizen, but most people would know Benjamin, the trader. My business has been such that I simply haven't had time for more than the required religious

23

activities. I admire those who do, but I just don't. Maybe when my son gets old enough to help me, I'll have more time for religious things, like discussing the Talmud and arguing the fine points of the law.

Sarah and I have a nice home in Jerusalem in one of the better sections of the city. However, even in the best sections of Jerusalem conditions are crowded. The houses are pushed up against one another. The buildings themselves are not very spacious, and the courtyards are really too small for any kind of garden. That's why we've always been glad we had a garden outside the city. It's not very far beyond the city wall—just a short walk. You go out toward the Mount of Olives, cross the brook Kidron and you're there. It's high enough on the Mount so you can look back and get quite a view of the city and the temple towers. Frankly, we've grown very fond of our garden. It's a haven for us. We can go out there and get away from the busyness of Jerusalem. Actually, it's not only a piece of luxury property either. There is a grove of olive trees on it, and we've built an olive press in one corner. Sarah and I like to eat the green olives with coarse brown bread. One tree yields about a thousand pounds of oil each year, which is more than enough for our family. So we're able to sell the oil from the other trees. We call our garden "Gethsemane." We put two words together—geth: meaning oil; and semane: meaning a plot or press. Because we have this little business out there, we have a wall around Gethsemane and keep the gates locked. But for me and my family it's not a business plot but a garden retreat. We've been happy to share our good fortune with friends. Quite a few of them have keys to the gate, and we've told them they can use the garden whenever they wish, and many of them do.

As a matter of fact, letting others use Gethsemane nearly got us into serious trouble. Let me tell you about it: One time I did an impulsive thing. My nature is to be rather cautious and careful, but this time I acted on impulse and lived to regret it. A young man from Nazareth came by and asked if he could have a key to my garden. He said he came to Jerusalem occasionally and wanted a spot where he could get off by himself. I understood how he felt. Sarah and I have held on to the property all these years because we had those same feelings. He seemed like a fine fellow—the kind you size up quickly as dependable and trustworthy. So, rather unwisely, without checking into his background any further, I

24

gave him a key. Apparently, he used the garden often when he was in Jerusalem. Some of the men who work for me at the oil press said they occasionally would find him there when they arrived early in the morning. It appeared to them he had spent the whole night. I couldn't see anything wrong with that. I'd often thought I'd be a better man if I got off by myself for long periods of solitude or meditation.

But, something wrong did happen and right there in my garden! It was during the Passover. If Jerusalem was crowded under normal conditions, you should have seen it at Passover time. Every square inch was occupied. On this particular evening, Sarah and I and the children had had our Passover meal and had gone to bed. Suddenly we were awakened by strange sounds outside the house. We were accustomed to hearing all sorts of odd noises when the city was crowded, but we could tell this was a different sort of sound. I threw something around me and ran up to the roof to see what was going on. Coming down the street were temple guards marching in formation. They were surrounded by a motley crew. You could call them a mob. As they passed beneath me, I noticed a man talking to the captain of the guard. I thought I recognized him. It took me a minute to place him, but then I remembered seeing him once with the man from Nazareth, Jesus. About that time I heard someone say what sounded like "Gethsemane." Gethsemane—good Lord! What could this mob have to do with Gethsemane?

I hurried down the stairs, put on some clothes, told Sarah what had happened, and ran out to the street to catch up with the mob. Sure enough, they headed out of the city right toward the Mount of Olives and my garden. They were a wild bunch. Some of them had had a bit too much wine. None of them seemed to know what was going on, but the guards did. It was obvious they were on an official mission and, whatever it was, the friend of the man from Nazareth was in on it, too.

When we got near Gethsemane, the gate was standing open, and I knew right away something was wrong. The friend of Jesus and the captain of the guard paused at the gate, then walked on in. The mob followed. The friend seemed to know right where he was going, as if he'd been there many times before. It was all sort of eerie and frightening. My garden looked and felt so different with the mob there. The spears of the guards flashed in the light of the blazing torches. And suddenly there he was. Ahead there a little was

25

Jesus, this man of Nazareth. He was kneeling, apparently in prayer. At the first sight of him, a hush passed over the mob. Then Jesus looked at us, stood up, and his friend went to him and kissed him. Immediately, the guards from the temple moved forward and surrounded him. They grabbed him and bound him as though he was a criminal. All the while he looked so peaceful and harmless. Then they turned to leave. By then the mob was milling about and beginning to shout again. I ran for the gate and waited. As they came through, the captain said to one of the crowd, "Who owns this garden anyway?" Someone said, "Benjamin, the trader," and, pointing in my direction added, "He's right over there." I wished the ground would open up and swallow me. Jesus glanced at me and nodded as if to say "thank you," but the captain came over and demanded, "What have you got to do with all of this?" All I could say was, "Nothing—nothing—I don't know anything about it." As the captain turned to leave, I shouted at his retreating back, "Believe me! I wasn't involved at all!"

THE PREACHER REFLECTS

We'll have to take Benjamin's word for it. He was not involved, at least not involved directly. Allowing Jesus to use his garden didn't mean that he endorsed his ideas or supported his cause. More than likely, Benjamin had no idea what this stranger from Nazareth thought or sought. Like thousands of good people in Jerusalem, he was not involved with Jesus in any way. And he was not involved with the temple guards either. If they were up to no good, he could not have known that. More than likely, Benjamin didn't have the vaguest notion why the priests would order such a man taken into custody. Benjamin, like thousands of good people of Jerusalem, was not involved in the temple's intrigue. Yet, we don't know whether to condemn Benjamin or to commend him. Should he have been involved? When some monstrous evil takes place in society, what should the good, moral, upright man be doing? Is it enough that he stand off at a distance, never quite coming out clearly for anything, never taking a stand with either side when issues are joined, never getting his hands dirty? When a monstrous evil takes place, is the good man to be commended for staying out of it and not getting mixed up in the mess? Or is he to be condemned for not being involved and refusing to get into it? Well, I choose to indict the uninvolved. Perhaps what I really want to do

26

is indict the idea that there is such a thing as an uninvolved man. For better or worse, every man is involved in the good and evil of society. We, you and I and Benjamin, may issue all the disclaimers we wish, but we are involved.

A HEIGHTENED SENSE OF GUILT

I think we need a heightened sense of guilt. I could have said we need a greater sense of responsibility, but that doesn't state the matter strongly enough. We need a heightened sense of guilt. The sins of society are our sins.

E. Stanley Jones tells of a visit to a city in China. The streets of the city were dirty and filthy, ankle deep in litter. The gentleman accompanying him said that it had been described as the dirtiest city in the world. To this companion, Dr. Jones said, "I don't understand this; these shops and stores are beautifully clean, Chinese gentlemen in them are dressed in silk, but these narrow streets are unspeakably dirty."

"It is easy to understand," [the man] replied; "for the shops and stores belong to these men, but the streets don't belong to anybody." With no sense of corporate responsibility, they "wallowed in corporate filth."[1] The sins of society, the filth and dirt of the streets, are our responsibility. The sins are ours; the streets are ours. It is not enough to keep our own little houses of life neat and in order. It is wrong to say that the streets belong to no one. They belong to everyone and everyone bears guilt for what happens in the streets.

A few short years ago, America was experiencing mass violence in the streets. Do you remember how you felt back in the days of violence and rioting? When all hell broke loose in Watts and Detroit and Washington, we were frightened, but many were self-righteous. We condemned violence, but all the while committed it. There were those who began to realize that the violence of the streets was an indirect, if not direct, result of the violence of the system. For scores of years, the system of which we have been a part has done violence to black people, robbed them of their human dignity, looted their will to achieve, destroyed their sense of worth. So Watts and Detroit and Washington rested on the conscience of all of us. We were all guilty—guilty of violence. Years ago, there

[1] E. Stanley Jones, *Christ and Human Suffering* (Nashville: Abingdon Press, 1933), pp. 182-183.

27

was a much publicized conference on religion and race held in Chicago. After days of discussing the problems, the time came for recommendations to the churches and Christian people of the land. And what was the suggestion? The first suggestion was, "Weep!" Weep in guilt and shame!

Back in Benjamin's day, there were good men who had nothing to do with starting the crucifixion or stopping it. They did not join the mob or seek to dissuade it. They did not support the power structure or resist it. But who could say that they were not responsible for what happened? "All that is necessary for the forces of evil to win the world," said someone, "is for enough good men to do nothing."[2] When good men think they are doing nothing, they are in fact doing something. They are tipping the scales in favor of evil. What happens in society is our responsibility, our fault. Issuing lame disclaimers will not absolve us. We need a heightened sense of guilt.

A HEIGHTENED SENSE OF WORTH

The good man in our society can feel so overwhelmed. The problems are so enormous. The evils are so monstrous. How can one man do anything? What could Benjamin have done? Would the course of events have been changed if one man had stood beside this Nazarene? Would the priests have listened to his pleading? Would the guards have paid any attention to him at all? The little guy, good though he may be, or even guilty as he may feel, seems so powerless—so worthless—in the face of the monstrous evils and the enormous problems of our day. We need a heightened sense of worth—the worth of the little guy, the solitary man.

A friend of mine says we've been taken in by one of the greatest hoaxes of all time. We've been taken in by the belief that the problems and evils of the world are beyond us. This *is* a hoax and we must identify it as a hoax.[3] There is nothing beyond our power to touch or to influence. Listen to these words from a book entitled *Hands Laid upon the Wind:*

> You say the little efforts that I make
> will do no good; they never will prevail

[2] Edmund Burke quoted by Paul L. Moore in *Seven Words of Men Around the Cross* (Abingdon Press, 1963), p. 44.

[3] Lloyd J. Averill, "The Significance of the Small," *Pulpit Digest* (February, 1966), p. 19.

to tip the hovering scale
where Justice hangs in balance.
I don't think
I ever thought they would.
But I am prejudiced beyond debate
in favor of my right to choose which side
shall feel the stubborn ounces of my weight.[4]

True, our weight may not tip the scales, but ours added to that of others will. Ours subtracted from others makes it that much more unlikely that good shall prevail. We need a heightened sense of worth to go along with a heightened sense of guilt. So to Benjamin we say: we believe you. You thought you weren't involved. But we believe you were wrong. You were involved.

The story of the cross is all about a man who became involved. He became involved with man and lost his life in the process. When we become involved with him, or when we become involved as he was in suffering service among men, we find life in the process.

[4] Bonaro W. Overstreet, *Hands Laid upon the Wind* (New York: W. W. Norton Company, 1955), p. 15. Reprinted by permission of W. W. Norton & Company, Inc. Copyright 1955 by W. W. Norton & Company, Inc.

3. Simon: Black Man with a Dream

Scripture: Matthew 27:27-32

SIMON SPEAKS

I can't remember when my dream was born. It was part of me for so long that I don't recall its beginning. My wife said it became an obsession with me, and I guess she was right. Perhaps only a Jew could fully understand it. But let me tell you about the dream, and what happened because of it.

My home is in Africa—North Africa. That explains the color of my skin. I live in Cyrene, a city on the Mediterranean coast. It's the capital of our country, Cyrenaica. I am a Jew, and that's a story in itself. I won't tell the whole story now, but years ago, when there was trouble in Jerusalem, a small group of Jews came to settle in our city. By the time I was born, the Jews had been in Cyrene many, many years. As I grew up, I was impressed by these people and their faith. Eventually I became one of them, and my family with me. I was determined to learn all I could about my new faith. I even changed my name so it sounded more Hebrew—Simon. My wife and I did everything we could to make ours a good Jewish home. We brought up our two boys, Rufus and Alexander, to be loyal sons of Abraham. The synagogue became our second home. It was there my dream was born. The older ones in our little congregation dreamed of Jerusalem. Some of them had been there; others longed to go there. For a Jew living anywhere in the world, Jerusalem was

31

the golden city, the center of the universe, the home of his faith. Each Jew hoped that sometime in his life he would make a pilgrimage to the holy city. And that became my dream. I dreamed I too would stand one day in the courts, would watch the sacrifices on the high altar. I can't remember just when, but there came a time when I started saving for my dream. Once, while housecleaning, my wife discovered the meager collection of coins I had hidden away. She smiled understandingly when I explained what they were. I was embarrassed. I could save so little. But I refused to give up my dream, and over the years a coin here and a coin there was added.

Then one day, quite unexpectedly, my opportunity came. A few of the members at the synagogue had decided the year had come to make their Passover pilgrimage to Jerusalem. It was not a minor matter. More than seven hundred miles lay between Cyrene and the holy city. These friends knew about my dream and asked if I would like to join them. Would I? That wasn't the question. The question was: Could I? I hadn't saved nearly enough for the whole family to make the trip and I was reluctant to go without them. Yet my wife urged me, saying it was my dream and another chance might be a long time coming. So, on the spur of the moment, the decision was made.

I wish I could tell you all about the journey. For a homebody like me, who'd never been far from the place of his birth, every day was full of excitement. But the greatest thrill was Jerusalem itself— especially the first glimpse of it. How can I describe it? There it was in all its splendor, my dream come true. It was even more wonderful than I had imagined. I could scarcely believe that I was there at last.

We had planned our arrival for early in the week of Passover. We wanted to be there in ample time to find lodging and to visit the historic places before the holy days began. I had my first disappointment soon after we got there. An African Jew, as it turned out, was something of an oddity, and no one wanted to rent me a room. I finally had to go out of the city to find a family willing to give me lodging. Each morning, I walked into the city and joined the others for the day's activities. Each night I went back out to rest. I wasn't happy about the arrangement, but the thrill of being there made up for some of my disappointment.

Actually, it was having to spend the nights outside the city

32

which led to my predicament. Friday morning I was on my way into Jerusalem. I was excited. Passover was drawing near. That day my friends and I planned to make final preparations for our sacrifices and our Passover meal. Those were the thoughts running through my mind when I began hearing noises. There, ahead of me, coming out of the city toward me, was a crowd. As it came closer, I saw Roman soldiers in the lead, followed by a noisy mob. Then I noticed the focus of the agitation was on three men. Each of them was carrying a heavy wooden beam. For a moment I didn't understand what was going on. Then it dawned on me: *These men are going to be crucified!* I'd heard about crucifixions but I'd never seen one. From what I had heard, I didn't want to see one. Just as the crowd reached me, one of the three victims stumbled and fell to the ground. Obviously, he had been badly abused. His back had been torn to shreds. Thorns had been jammed down on his head. His face was a bloody mess. The soldier in charge kicked at his side while he lay there in the dust and ordered him to stand. He struggled to his feet, but when he tried to pick up the wooden beam he fell again. I shuddered at the sight of such cruelty. I'd seen all I wanted to see and turned to leave. I thought, *how could men do such things to each other?* And then, just as if a rock had hit me in the back, I heard a rough voice, "You there, you black man, come carry this wood for this weakling here." I had no choice. Who does, with Roman spears at his back? But why me? Why me? And there went my dream. Years of hoping and saving, miles of traveling, days of walking, and one touch of wood with this man's blood on it and I would be unclean—not able to share in the Passover. Why me? Because I am black, of course. Why else? The soldier didn't dare ask a local Jew. He knew the rules about ritual cleanliness. He didn't dare offend one of the local Jews. But a black man—that was different.

So I carried the beam. I was there in the middle of the mob. I heard all the abuse, all the obscenity heaped on the three of them and especially on the one. I'll never forget my own terror and I wasn't even one of the victims. That mob was eager to see blood spilled. And the man whose wood I was carrying—I didn't know what to think about him at the time. Different? Unique? Unusual? Yes. Criminal? No, I didn't think so.

When we got to the spot where the execution was to take place, I dropped the wood to the ground. I rubbed my aching shoulder. My

33

hand came away bloody. It was his blood, not mine. The horror of what happened during the next few minutes will never be erased from my memory. Those Romans were experts at their trade— inflicting pain. Finally, when the crosses were in position and the slow death under way, I couldn't take my eyes off "my man," as I called him. Never once did he cry out angrily or resist. Never once did he curse. After a while, I noticed his lips moving. I went closer to catch anything he might say. I thought I heard him say something like, "Father, forgive them." I stumbled away. Three men were dying. My dream was dead. *Why*, I asked, *do men do this to each other? When will it stop? When will men stop destroying one another? I wish it would stop right now!*

THE PREACHER REFLECTS

We must confess to Simon that it has not stopped. We still abuse one another. We persist in destroying each other. With each generation since his we have become increasingly clever and sophisticated in perpetrating inhumanities on one another. Yes, it ought to stop, but it has not stopped yet!

I once heard a great preacher say that mankind customarily hates the exceptionally good and the exceptionally bad. Man is embarrassed by the exceptionally bad and shamed by the exceptionally good, so both are put out of the way. Jesus, the exceptionally good, was crucified between two thieves, the exceptionally bad. There is substantial truth in this preacher's hypothesis. Each of us could make his own study of history to test it out. However, there may be a truth even more elemental and universal than this distaste for the exceptionally good and bad. It is something to which our attention is directed by Simon of Cyrene.

We abuse the different. We dislike or distrust the different. If that puts the case too strongly, we could overwork the word itself and say we feel differently about the different. Jesus was different. He was not bad. His enemies watched him carefully for evidence of wrongdoing and found none. Even Pilate said, "I find no fault in him at all." He was different. Simon also was different. As far as we know, he was neither exceptionally good nor exceptionally bad. In North Africa, he would have been just one of the crowd. But, outside Jerusalem his was a black face in a sea of white faces. He was different.

Think with me about how you and I relate to the different. In

34

this world, there are lots of things that ought to stop and stop now! All racial injustices in whatever form ought to stop! All killing by whatever name—war, murder, capital punishment—ought to stop! However, it is useful for us to think about the things that ought to stop or start in us. Rather than wander around over the surface of the great issues facing society, we can focus on us and our own feelings. Here are simple suggestions about things we must do in relating to the different.

PROMISE TO BE PERSONAL

That soldier who conscripted Simon did not see a person. He looked over the crowd and saw a black face. To him, all black faces belonged in a certain category. He did not see a person—the father of two sons, Rufus and Alexander; a dreamer of dreams; a pilgrim of devout faith. He saw a category, not a person. All black men were such and such, therefore each black man could be treated thus and so. Yet Simon was a person. To how many in that unruly mob was Jesus a person? Not very many, if any. No, he was a threat to be eliminated, a problem to be solved, a nuisance to be eradicated.

In Jesus' day and in ours, men are prone to deal with one another in categories or by categories. Let a person come along who is a little different, not like us in the shade of his skin or the shape of his ideas, and we immediately classify him. Then, once we've placed him in a convenient category, it isn't necessary for us to think of him as a person. Most of our hates are "label hates," someone has said.[1] In Jesus' day, the people of Cana said, "Could any good thing come out of Nazareth?" and the people of Nazareth said, "Could any good thing come out of Cana?" A Gentile might have said, "The only good Jew is a dead Jew." Pharisees said, "All publicans are sinners, all harlots are to be damned, all Samaritans are outcasts." They labeled and hated, and we do the same. Rather than know a man's name we would like to know where he fits. Is he black or white, liberal or conservative, hawk or dove, Republican or Democrat, Protestant or Catholic or Jew? Once we know where he fits, we can deal with him much more easily. We don't even have to think about it. We have a standard response for all Negroes, all hawks, all Democrats, all Jews. We categorize and deal with one another. We label and hate.

[1]Glenn Clark, *The Way, the Truth and the Life* (New York: Harper & Row, Publishers, 1946), p. 34.

35

A few years ago, some students at Barnard and Columbia, in New York City, were shown photographs of thirty attractive young women. The photos were unmarked, unlabeled, unnamed. The students were asked to rank them according to beauty. Records were kept of the rankings. Two months later, the same students were shown the same photographs, but this time names were attached. The names were fictitious, with obvious national origins—Polish names, German names, and so forth. The students were asked to rank the photos by the same criteria as earlier. However, this time the placements were radically different than before. Those photos with "different" sounding names were ranked lowest. We label and lose the person.[2]

In *Future Shock*, the much talked about book by Alvin Toffler, the story of a unique people is told. Not far from Route 80, outside the little town of Hazard, Kentucky, there is a place known as the Valley of Troublesome Creek. In that tiny, backwoods community lives a family whose members for generations have been marked by a strange anomaly. Their skin is blue. A doctor from the University of Kentucky College of Medicine tracked down the story and discovered the family to be perfectly normal in every other way. Yet they have blue skin. He concluded that the unusual coloration was caused by a rare enzyme deficiency passed from one generation to another. Toffler says that with our fast accumulating knowledge of genetics we will soon be able to breed whole new races of people— blue, green, purple, orange, and such.[3] Consider this: If it was our decision to make, would we create just one color? Would it be better if everyone was just like you, or me? Or, are we big enough, human enough, intelligent enough, Christian enough to enjoy all the differences? If we could be personal, we would not want everyone to be alike, nor hurry to put all blacks, all blues, all Baptists, all Roman Catholics into convenient categories where we handle them without thinking.

Each man is a person, not a unit of a category. Each man has a name, not a label. Each man is an individual, not a specimen of a species. It was said of St. Francis that he deliberately did not see the forest for the trees, nor the mob for the men. When that can be said

[2] This incident is discussed in an article by Robert L. Heilbroner, "Don't Let Stereotypes Warp Your Judgment," *Reader's Digest*, vol. 80, no 477 (January, 1962), pp. 66-68.

[3] Alvin Toffler, *Future Shock* (New York: Random House, Inc., 1970), p. 179.

of each of us, we shall have begun to keep our promise to be personal.

DARE TO BE DIFFERENT

Thus far we have suggested that we owe each man his personhood. Now we go a step further to suggest that we owe ourselves individuality. We must dare to be different and glory in our individuality. Simon was different. He was a black man, but that is just the beginning. He was a Jew, perhaps the only black man in the synagogue at Cyrene. However, that is still just the beginning. He became a Christian; at least I'm assuming that. In the book of Acts, chapter 13, verse 1, Simon is mentioned again. That time he is identified as a black man and a Christian. I like Simon for that reason. Certainly I like him for helping the weary Jesus, but I like him especially because he dared to be different. He dared to think for himself and to stand on his own two feet.

If it is wrong for me to condemn a person to life in a category, it is equally wrong for me to surrender my individuality to the mind of the masses. Even as I promise to avoid treating others by categories, I refuse to be captured by a category. I will not be just another WASP—a White Anglo-Saxon Protestant. When people talk about the prevailing attitude in my city or neighborhood, I refuse to be so categorized. I insist on being an individual. Remember what Thoreau said as a boy of eight? He was asked what he was going to be when he grew up and replied, "I'll be I."

Most of us shudder when we remember the goose-stepping Nazis of the Second World War. How, we ask, could a nation be so misled? Why didn't individuals stand up and be counted? When my family was in Germany several summers ago, my wife and I found ourselves looking at the people our age or older and wondering: Where were you? What did you do? Yet it is so easy for us to surrender our individuality, to fall into step. It is so easy for us to think like everyone else is thinking, to do what everyone else is doing. We owe ourselves better treatment than that. We owe ourselves individuality. The least we can do in this age as Christians is promise to be personal and dare to be different.

We confess to Simon that it is true—sad, but true. Man's inhumanity to man has not stopped yet. However, I am determined that it will stop at least in my life. That's why I promise to be personal and dare to be different.

37

4. Claudia: Wife with a Nightmare

Scripture: Matthew 27:11-23

CLAUDIA SPEAKS

He was a handsome one when I married him. He cut quite a figure as a Roman officer. The sight of him caused many a maid's heart to flutter. Yet I wouldn't say I loved Pilate at first sight, or that our marriage was a passionate romance. Actually, it was more like an advantageous arrangement for both of us. He was ambitious, anxious to move on to higher rank and better things. I had connections and could open doors for him. He had a kind of rugged ability but he lacked polish. His disposition was of a blustery sort, and he frequently bungled his way into difficult situations. With my background I thought I could help him. You see, I grew up among the aristocrats. My mother was the third wife of Tiberius Caesar. I was a granddaughter of Caesar Augustus. So I knew my way around Rome and had friends in high places. Better still, I knew from the inside how the Caesars managed to get and use power.

So Pilate and I were married. His blustery ambition and my aristocratic know-how joined forces. Some time later the first big opportunity came our way. The governorship in Judea was available. It wasn't exactly a choice assignment. Judea had the reputation of being a real trouble spot. Yet the position of procurator anywhere in the empire was not to be frowned upon.

39

Further, if a man could do a good job in such a difficult place, it might lead quickly to better things.

Pilate and I talked it over. I spoke to the right people, and the appointment was his. There was a regulation prohibiting wives from joining their husbands at such a remote post, but again, my connections helped and we went together. Truthfully, I was afraid to let Pilate go out there alone. I was certain he would blunder into one crisis after another.

My fears were well founded. Even with me at his side, he was in trouble almost from the hour we arrived. For example, Pilate, like any good Roman procurator, displayed a bust of Caesar. The Jews, it seemed, had scruples against displaying images of any men. Caiaphas, their high priest, insisted that the bust be removed. My husband said, "No!" I thought Pilate was stubborn, but you should have seen those Jews. They were beyond reason, fanatical about the matter. Within hours we had a revolt on our hands. Finally Pilate had to back down. I've never seen him so furious. And there were other things that happened too. You always had the feeling you were sitting on a volcano which might erupt at any moment. We were especially uneasy on the Jewish high holy days. Overnight Jerusalem was crowded with people, all of them milling about. My husband had learned by experience to double the guard in key locations around the city because minor disturbances would break out here and there.

Jerusalem was like that—crowded and excited—the night Caiaphas came to the palace. It was a Thursday night. Pilate and I were talking together in our favorite chamber, a comfortable sitting room. One of the servants appeared and announced the arrival of Caiaphas. We both were surprised. It wasn't like the high priest to pay a social call. We surely were not bosom friends. Further, during high holy days the priests were kept busy with ceremonial chores. Pilate suggested I retire to my quarters. With some apprehension and considerable curiosity, he went to greet his unexpected visitor. In my room I waited—and waited—and waited. It seemed like a long, long time before Pilate joined me.

He told me Caiaphas had come to bargain with him. There was a young troublemaker they wanted out of the way. He was putting dangerous ideas into the people's heads and was disrupting normal operations at the temple. They had had difficulty getting evidence against the man, but one of his own followers had given

40

them what they needed. Their plan was to take him into custody later that same night, question him, and then bring him to the procurator for trial. Caiaphas wanted Pilate's promise that the man would be tried and convicted. I asked, "But what do they have against him?" Pilate said, "They claim they have enough, and they're determined to go through with it." "It doesn't sound right to me," I said, "and you know how Tiberius feels about convicting innocent men." "Yes," he answered, "but Caiaphas has threatened to send word to Tiberius about all the troubles we've had here and to request my replacement. That would mean the end of me." "So you promised him?" I asked. "Yes, Claudia, I promised. What else could I do?"

That was a bad night for me. I tossed and turned all night long. When I did sleep, I had horrible dreams about my husband being stripped of his rank and humiliated—dreams about troubles with Caiaphas—dreams about this innocent man, whoever he was, and what they were planning to do with him. When the maid entered my room in the morning, she found me exhausted from a restless night. She had been with me many years and knew me well. She sensed that I was troubled. So, while she brushed my hair, I told her all about the strange happenings of the night before. When I finished the story, she said, "His name is Jesus. I've seen him. To me he seems kind and gentle. As a matter of fact, one of the men working in the kitchen here in the palace has a relative who was healed by him." "Really?" I exclaimed. "Is that the kind of person he is? Is that the man they want out of the way?" Her comments, added to my miserable night, left me in a great distress. When I finished dressing, I rushed to my husband's room, only to find him gone. His servant said he had been summoned to court very early. I thought, "Oh, no, they've started the Jesus trial already. They didn't waste any time." Hurriedly I wrote a note. I knew it was most irregular and probably would embarrass my husband, but I had to get a message to him. I wrote, "Pilate, please reconsider. If you think this man may be innocent, don't act hastily. I've heard he's a good man, and I've worried all night about this matter." The servant raced off with the note. He returned in a few minutes saying he had delivered it safely into my husband's hand. He added that Pilate read it immediately and heaved a heavy sigh.

When Pilate got home later, he looked so tired and defeated. I started to speak, but he held up his hand to stop me. "I know how

41

you feel, Claudia, but I had no choice. They said he was guilty and they were not going to take 'no' for an answer. I even offered them a substitute, Barabbas. But they wanted Jesus. Well, they've got him. He is on his way now to crucifixion. I hope they're satisfied." I could hardly speak. You know how women are, with premonitions and all that. I had the terrible feeling my husband had just made the worst mistake of his life. He slumped to the couch in exhaustion. I went over to him, cradled his head in my lap, and said to myself, *Poor Pilate, you think your troubles are over. I have the feeling they've just begun. I hope I'm wrong. By all the gods, I hope I'm wrong.*

THE PREACHER REFLECTS

Claudia was right. Her fears were founded. Her wifely premonitions were confirmed. Her husband did make a mistake, a colossal mistake.

Pilate allowed a gross miscarriage of justice to take place. It is rather sad that the major remembrance of a man's career could be caught up in a single phrase in the Apostles' Creed. It says a man named Jesus "suffered under Pontius Pilate." If it were not for this one major mistake in his life, Pilate's name would be known only by the rare specialist in ancient history. Because of that mistake, he lives on in something akin to infamy. "Poor Pilate." He's a tragic sort of character.

There has been considerable conjecture about the effect that all of this had on Claudia and Pilate. Did Claudia ever forget her awful nightmares? Did Pilate really feel absolved of responsibility? Did their consciences ever bother them at all? It is conceivable that Claudia and Pilate soon forgot this unfortunate incident and satisfactorily pushed it from their minds. We might imagine Pilate writing a report to his superiors back in Rome. Perhaps he included reference to the Jewish holy days and the consequent need for additional military personnel to keep the peace. But what do you think he might have written about this Jesus business? Would he have mentioned it at all? Would he have noted the three crucifixions and passed them off as inconsequential? Maybe he reasoned that a few Jews, more or less, would never be missed. Do you suppose that it bothered Pilate and Claudia no more than that?

There is a legend that says it bothered them much more than that. Near Lucerne, in Switzerland, there is a mountain named

42

after Pilate, Mount Pilatus. The legend says that often in the moonlight the figure of Pilate can be seen emerging from the waters of Lake Lucerne in the shadow of the mountain. The ghost of Pilate forever moans, forever groans, forever washes his hands. I've been there, but on that ghostly sort of day the lake and mountain were lost in thick, heavy fog. I heard no moaning, no groaning. Do you suppose it bothered Pilate and Claudia that much?

There is a tradition that says it bothered them into belief. The Greek church holds that Claudia became a Christian, and a Christian of such devotion that she was beatified—made into a saint. The Coptic or Egyptian Church honors both Claudia and Pilate, considering him a martyr and a saint. Do you suppose that it bothered them so much that they were in fact bothered into belief?

The truth is that we are relegated to just that: supposing. We don't know precisely what happened to either Claudia or Pilate. Yet somehow we feel that life was never quite the same for them. Further, we believe that life is never quite the same for any person who truly confronts Jesus Christ. Jesus was on trial before Pilate, to be sure. But in a far more profound sense Pilate was on trial before Jesus. And it always shall be so: Men confront Jesus; they cannot avoid him. Men are on trial before Jesus; they cannot evade him. I think there are things to be learned from all of this. We can't be certain that Pilate and Claudia learned them, but that's no reason why we should not learn them. We cannot avoid encounter with Jesus; neither can we evade him.

ENCOUNTER WAS AND IS INEVITABLE

Sooner or later, Pilate and Jesus were bound to meet. Eventually, inevitably, they had to meet. In some western melodramas it was said of two men that the town or territory wasn't big enough for the two of them. Sooner or later a showdown between them was inevitable. Well, in a way Palestine wasn't big enough for Pilate and Jesus. At least it was small enough that sooner or later they had to confront one another. Encounter was inevitable. The Scriptures picture Pilate trying to avoid that. He employed a number of diversionary tactics to avoid a face-to-face confrontation, but all of them failed. At last they were there together, face-to-face. There was no way to get out of it. Encounter was inevitable.

43

Encounter is inevitable. Sooner or later every man meets Jesus. The world is not big enough for any man to avoid him. Eventually, inevitably, encounter takes place. Let me try to explain what I mean by that. I don't mean that every man sometime in his life is compelled either to reject or accept the claims of Christ as Lord, or the claims that the church has made for him. I don't mean that every person will accept or reject Jesus as Master and Savior. There are still people who live and die on this earth who have not heard the name of Jesus. Yet I believe that in a sense they encounter him, know him or not.

Follow this reasoning: Jesus said, "I am the truth" (John 14:6). If he is the truth, how can a man avoid him? He didn't mean he was scientific truth or mathematical truth. He wasn't the truth about nuclear fission and such. He was the truth about life and the living of life. If so, then anything that has life, any living human, inevitably faces him as he faces life. It has been said that Jesus is not a preference.[1] We know about preferences. I prefer coffee, you prefer tea; another prefers hot chololate, another cola, etc. There is no truth that determines what we should drink. It is simply a matter of individual taste and preference. But Jesus is truth, not preference or personal taste. Whether I like it or not, whether you like it or not, regardless of my preferences, regardless of your preferences, he is truth. He is truth about life, about the living of human life. Every man, by the simple fact of his living, encounters the Christ truth. He lives challenging the Christ truth or defending the Christ truth. Life works the Jesus way. One lives with the grain or against the grain.

Let me put this in another way: Profanity is to me a strange, amusing, and lamentable phenomenon. I suspect that the name of Jesus Christ is uttered as much as any two words in the English language. All kinds of people, some of them religious, and others far from it, use great quantities of profanity. The most non-religious, nonspiritual, thoroughly pagan person may find it impossible to speak more than two sentences without using the name of Jesus Christ. I'm not condoning profanity, but I find it amusing that so few can avoid using the name of Jesus. In the same sort of way, I don't think that a person can live two hours without

---

[1] D. T. Niles, *That They May Have Life* (New York: Harper & Row, Publishers, 1951), p. 18.

44

confronting Jesus Christ. He may not know it. He may deny it, but it's true. The Christ principles, the Christ truths are inescapable.[2] Let a man try to avoid Jesus in his home and he creeps in through love and selflessness. Let a man try to avoid him in his business and he creeps in through service and ethics and interpersonal relations. Let a man try to avoid him in society and he creeps in to judge and to make a godless world tremble and shake. A man may not know it, a man may not name it, but he cannot avoid it. Pilate teaches us that encounter was and is inevitable.

EVASION WAS AND IS IMPOSSIBLE

Sooner or later Pilate had to make some kind of decision about Jesus. The Scriptures picture him as trying to evade it. He thrusts him back on Caiaphas, sends him over to Herod, suggests a substitute in Barabbas. When all else fails, in a sort of ultimate attempt at evasion, he washes his hands. Nonsense. Jesus was delivered into his hands. Evasion was impossible.

Evasion is impossible. I'm addressing this part to the Christians. The first observation about encounter's inevitability was for non-Christians. This second observation is for us Christians. Jesus is in our hands as he was in Pilate's . What will we do with him? Back then everyone tried to make it someone else's affair. Herod insisted it was not his affair. Claudia didn't want it to be her husband's affair. No one wanted to make it his own affair. But Jesus is our affair. He has been delivered into our hands. We may try evasion: let someone else make a decision about him; let someone else take him seriously; let someone else try to live by his principles; let someone else try to elevate the morality of society. Let the preacher do our witnessing and the church school teacher our Bible study. Let the schools teach values to our children. Let the courts desegregate our society. Let the Congress legislate elemental justice. Let Pilate, let Herod, let Caiaphas, let anyone else do it. Let anyone else take Jesus seriously. What will we do? We wash our hands of it!

But Jesus is in our hands, yours and mine, fellow Christians. He has been delivered into our hands. He is our affair. What will we do with him? Will we take him seriously or pass him off lightly? This

[2]Ralph W. Sockman discusses this idea in *The Unemployed Carpenter* (New York: Harper & Row, Publishers, 1933), p. 63.

45

is one we Christians can't sit out. We either crown him or crucify him. Evasion was and is impossible.

John Masefield created a scene that's a favorite of mine. It is in his poetic drama *The Trial of Jesus*. Longinus, a Roman soldier, has come to report to Pilate about the empty tomb. Procula meets him and they talk. They discuss the claim that Jesus has risen from the dead and whether or not that claim is at all believable. Procula asks Longinus, "Do you think he is dead?" Longinus replies, "No, lady, I don't!" "Then where is he?" asks Procula. "Let loose in the world, lady, where neither Roman nor Jew can stop his truth."[3]

That is it precisely: Jesus is loose in the world. We cannot avoid him. We cannot evade him. What shall we do with him?

[3] John Masefield, *The Trial of Jesus* (Boston: Baker's Plays, 1925), p. 59.

5. Miriam: Maid with an Eye

Scripture: Mark 14:53-72

MIRIAM SPEAKS

That day began like any other day. Leah, Rachel, and I were up bright and early to begin our household chores. We had worked together for years and had our own routine for getting things done. The master of the household wasn't the easiest person in the world to work for. He was the high priest. Caiaphas was his name. As you might guess, he was a demanding sort of person. Let me tell you though, there were worse places a maid could work. The high priest didn't live in poverty. Far from it. The house was one of the finest in Jerusalem and one of the largest. It was built around an open courtyard. Caiaphas and his family lived on the second floor and, frankly, they wanted for nothing. Those of us who served the family had our quarters on the first floor, and those servant quarters were better than the homes of most people. In the kitchen we prepared only the best foods; in the laundry we washed delicate fabrics and lovely lace; in dusting we handled costly, precious things. Caiaphas was the kind who had to have things just so, and all of us were slightly afraid of him. Yet I didn't want to work for anyone else. The household of a high priest was an exciting place! When my father got me the job, I was delighted. I thought I would be where lots of fascinating things happened—and I was right.

I don't mean every day was a thrilling adventure. Perhaps it

47

sounds odd for me to say it, but a priest's house gets as dirty as any other; his clothes require as much scrubbing as any man's; his dishes have to be washed like everybody else's. A maid is a maid in any household. There were many days that were plain, ordinary, dull working days. On such days, our only diversion was the visit of a merchant or the arrival of a delivery. There was one big, burly visitor we always enjoyed. He teased us and we kidded him. Simon was his name. He brought fish to the kitchen often, and each time he brightened our day and gave us something to laugh about. Then, for no apparent reason, he stopped coming and someone else made the fish deliveries. We heard rumors about him. We were told he had become quite religious and was following a teacher from Nazareth. Supposedly he was a completely different person and had changed his name from Simon to Peter. We maids found it hard to believe that rough and ready Simon could ever be very religious. I mention him because he was involved in the day I began to tell you about.

As I said, that day began like other days. Oh, there was extra activity because of Passover, but we were used to that. However, as the day wore on, I had the feeling something out of the ordinary was afoot. People were coming and going all day. Members of the Sanhedrin went up to our master's rooms for hurried conferences and then left in haste. Caiaphas was much more agitated than usual. When Leah came back from serving the noon meal, she said, "Watch your step. He's really out of sorts today." There seemed to be an ominous mood hovering over the household. We maids were glad when the last chore was done and we could go to our quarters for some women-type talk. But, as it turned out, the day was far from over.

We were beginning to relax when we heard heavy pounding on the courtyard door. I volunteered to go see what it was and was greeted by a group of temple guards. Without waiting to be asked, they barged right in. The captain of the guard headed for the stairs up to the high priest's quarters. The others just made themselves comfortable around the courtyard as best they could. The captain wasn't upstairs long. He came down and said to his men, "Come on. Judas will meet us outside the city wall." And off they went. Bewildered, I latched the door and went back to join the other girls. We must have talked for an hour or so and were ready to go to sleep when suddenly the street outside was full of noise. Again there was

48

a heavy bang on the courtyard door. This time Leah answered it. The next thing I knew, the courtyard was alive with people. I saw a few of the temple guards going up the steps, pushing someone ahead of them. He was bound like a prisoner. Then Leah came back and said, "Let's go, girls. Those men out there want a fire and something hot to drink." So out we went.

Before long a fire was going. The men were warming themselves and sipping hot broth. The courtyard had quieted down. Meanwhile, upstairs, things were far from quiet. I thought one of us should see if Caiaphas wanted anything served up there. So I started for the steps. As I did, the courtyard door slowly opened. Apparently Leah had forgotten to latch it. A man slipped in, acting suspiciously. He startled me at first, but I went on. Halfway up the steps, I stopped and whirled around. *That was Simon! The man who slipped in was Simon. What's he doing here?* I thought. I went on up. I wish I hadn't. I approached the door, looked in, and froze in my steps. What they were doing to that man! Caiaphas was shaking with rage. One guard blindfolded and struck the prisoner. Then another struck him and they all laughed. I tore myself away, hurried down the steps, and found Rachel. When I told her what was going on upstairs, she said, "You realize that's that Jesus." "What Jesus?" I asked. "Oh, you know," she said, "that fellow Simon is supposed to have followed." "Oh, no," I said, "that explains it!" "Explains what?" she asked. "Why Simon is here, of course." "Simon, here?" Rachel said. "Are you sure? I haven't seen him. Where is he?" "I can't be positive," I answered, "but I think I saw him. Let me see if I can find him."

I found him all right, standing in a shadow. He didn't hear me approach. I watched him for a few minutes. His eyes were fixed on the room upstairs where all the noise was coming from. He was straining to see and hear all he could. I said softly, "Simon?" He made no response. Then I remembered about his new name and said a little louder, "Peter?" He jumped with a start. "Peter, are you one of his followers?" He tried to act as if he didn't know me, but I said, "Simon, you can't fool me. I'm Miriam. Remember? You can change your name to Peter, but I'd still know you anywhere. Were you with him? Really, are you one of that man's followers?" By this time some others had gathered about us. He looked at me as if to beg, "Please, Miriam, leave me alone." Then he said, "Woman, I don't even know that man." But I kept on. I had to know. "Then

49

why are you here? You have no business being here. You must be one of his followers!" "Woman," he said, "you are wrong. I am not one of his followers." Others began joining in. They taunted him and teased him and tried to make a fool of him. I was sorry I had started the whole affair. I watched as Peter buried his head in his hands while the jeering and taunting went on. Then he let out an oath. It was something he must have learned among the fishermen. He screamed it out, and with his outburst everyone stopped their noisemaking. Peter added with a shout, "I tell you I do not know the man and do not know what you are talking about." There was dead silence. From somewhere a long way off, a cock's crowing cut through the chilly morning air—and Peter cried. Big, burly Simon cried. I couldn't believe my eyes. That strong, giant of a man was crying. He turned and ran out through the doorway.

I watched him go. He had convicted himself. Of course he was one of the man's followers. Nothing could be more obvious. What kind of person was this Jesus who could affect big, strong Simon like that? I glanced upstairs and heard the horseplay still going on and wondered what kind of man was bad enough to be treated like that. I slipped into my room and sat on my bed. I thought about all the happenings of the day and the night. I thought about Caiaphas: mad; the guards: cruel; this man from Nazareth: misused; and Simon, or Peter, or whatever he wants to call himself: crying! I said to myself, *Maybe a maid isn't supposed to be able to figure people out, but believe me, I've seen all kinds.*

THE PREACHER REFLECTS

Miriam saw her share of life and many kinds of men. There are many kinds to see, many kinds of religious men to see, and she saw her share of them that night. If she was confused about this matter of religious men, it certainly is understandable.

Caiaphas was a religious man. He had reached the very top of the priestly profession. He must have been an impressive sight robed in his vestments. He was a man of power and prestige. Jesus was a religious man, too. He was in nearly complete contrast to Caiaphas. He wore the plainest of peasant's garb. He had no position, no prestige, and no place to lay his head. How could two men, so different, so diametrically opposed, both be religious? Then there was Peter. As Miriam told the story, she had little difficulty identifying Peter, but she did have trouble thinking of him as religious. He was a big, rocklike hulk of a man, full of the rich juices of life. He was reduced to an angry, sulky, weeping man. Was it that change that marked him as religious?

There they are: Caiaphas, Jesus, and Peter—three kinds of men, three kinds of religious men. In light of that, what kind of a man is a religious man? What kind of a man is a Christian? Should it be possible to identify the Christian, to pick him out of any group? Should Christians be a readily recognizable kind of people? Every Christian, I think, lives with the feeling that he ought somehow to be visible. Peter was visible. With his Galilean garb and Galilean accent, everyone knew he was different. It was plain for all to see that he was out of place there in the high priest's courtyard. We Christians wear the same clothes as everyone else. We speak the same language. We would be reluctant to don a uniform or wear a badge. Yet we know we ought by some means to be visible. Let's assume that a Christian kind of man should have some identifying marks. Perhaps there are insights here in this story of Miriam and Peter that can be instructive for us.

A Christian kind of man is identifiable:

NOT BECAUSE OF HIS CHARACTER,
BUT BECAUSE OF HIS COMPANION.

That may seem an awkward way to express it, but there is justification for it. The thing that marked Peter as unmistakably Christian was the fact that he was there with Jesus. He was there in the courtyard, there for no reason except that Jesus was there. He was there *where,* there *when* Jesus was. That is what convinced the others he was Christian. Miriam said, "Peter, you've been with him, haven't you?" Read again the Four Gospels. See how each describes this courtyard scene and discover in each that the damning evidence against Peter is the same: he had been with Jesus. We know more about Peter than any other disciple. We have sufficient references in the New Testament to have a fairly detailed picture of the person he was. We know considerable about his personality, his strengths and weaknesses, his moods. However, he was identified as a Christian, not because of his character, but because of his companion.

Watch twelve men walk down a Palestinian path. Who are they? What are they? Can you tell? No, but put Jesus there with them, and you know immediately. These are the twelve disciples. It is not

51

their appearance or character but their companion that marks them.

In any Christian congregation there is every conceivable type or kind of personality. There are the nice and the nasty, the charitable and the not so charitable, the bright and cheery and the gloomy and sour, the introverts and the extroverts, the childish and the mature. Yet all are nominal Christians. We are many kinds, yet Christian. The thing that identifies us as Christians is not our personality type but the presence of a Person. What makes us Christian is the presence of Christ in our lives. Are we, or are we not, with Jesus?

An idea expressed by C. S. Lewis is helpful to me at this point. Imagine two people: Miss Bates, who is a Christian and has a nasty tongue; Dick Firkin, who is not a Christian and has a kind tongue. How do you explain that? Well, the real question is what Miss Bate's tongue would be like if she were not a Christian and what Dick's tongue would be like if he were. Lewis says that what Christianity proposes to do is to put the temperaments of both Miss Bates and Dick Firkin under new management.[1] When Christ takes over the management of a person's life, that life may be in any condition of repair or disrepair. It is not the momentary condition of his life, good or bad, that identifies him as Christian. Rather, it is the fact that he is under new management. It is the fact that Christ is now present there. We must add that Christ is not content to allow us to remain in the same condition of repair or disrepair in which he finds us. If today we are as nasty as when we became Christians, then there is serious question as to whether or not we have been with Jesus. It is a truism that we become like that with which we spend a great deal of time. If we have made little or no progress in becoming Christlike, then perhaps we have not been with Jesus enough. What identifies us as Christians is not the condition of our lives at this moment, but the fact that together with Jesus we are headed somewhere with them. A Christian kind of man is identifiable, not because of his character at the moment, but because of his Companion of a lifetime.

Further, a Christian kind of man is identifiable:

NOT BECAUSE HE IS PERFECT,
BUT BECAUSE HE IS PERFECTLY HONEST.

[1] C. S. Lewis, *Mere Christianity* (New York: The Macmillan Company, 1952), p. 163.

52

This is similar to what has been said thus far, but a necessary element is added. Peter was far from perfect. Miriam knew that and wondered how a fellow such as he could be a religious person. Further, Peter's honesty may be in question in light of his flat denial of Jesus in the courtyard. Yet, before we are too harsh on Peter, we need to ask about the source of this story of the denials. Scholars generally agree that the book of Mark is the oldest of the gospels. They agree also that the book of Mark largely contains the preaching of Peter. If so, then Peter told this story about himself. It seems likely that he himself used it in his preaching. It is doubtful if Miriam wrote up the incident and submitted a manuscript for publication. Peter told the story. He was not perfect, but he was perfectly honest. I can imagine Peter telling and retelling this story in perfect honesty. "I am not perfect. I let my Lord down. I denied him and deserted him, but look what the grace of God has done with me!"

As we noted earlier, there is every kind of personality in every congregation. But there is not one single perfect person in any congregation. That shouldn't come as a shock or revelation to anyone. Not one of us is perfect. One does not have to be perfect to be Christian, but he should be perfectly honest. The Christian is that kind of person who in perfect honesty knows the sort of fourteen-carat scoundrel he is—a sinner, not able on his own to be anything but a sinner. That perfect honesty becomes an invitation to God's grace. Grace is surely the missing element in the religious experience of many of us. We are busy being good or busy trying to be good. We are hard at work trying to be as perfect as possible. We forget that what is required is not perfection but perfect honesty with ourselves and God. Until we stop presenting God with our meager attempts at perfection and instead present him our perfect honesty as sinners, we shall know no grace.

There is a little fun-type book called *Games Christians Play*. It is by its own admission "an irreverent guide to religion without tears." In the preface it claims to be a handbook for the Christian on "how to live like the devil and still be a saint."[2] Well, that may require a handbook, but I don't think that's our problem. I think our problem is that we think we must try desperately to live like a saint and we feel like the devil. We try, or think we must try, to do

[2] Judi Culbertson and Patti Bard, *Games Christians Play* (New York: Harper & Row, Publishers, 1967), p. 7.

53

good, to be good and perfect. That's a burdensome chore. How much better it would be if, rather than try to save ourselves and present God with a finished, perfected product, we presented ourselves as we honestly are and let him save us. Then perhaps we could relax and enjoy the good works we do. It is not our goodness that makes us Christians. It is God's grace. Only a sinner needs grace—only an acknowledged sinner feels grace.

A Christian kind of man is identifiable, not because of his character at the moment, but because of his Companion of a lifetime; not because he is perfect, but because he is perfectly honest.

Have you ever watched an academic procession and tried to determine who's who and what's what? The academic gowns come in a variety of styles. There are different colors, different hoods—some have stripes on the sleeves, some no sleeves. And the people themselves are an assorted group, too—some old, some young, some men, some women, some big, some small. The truth is that scholars come in assorted sizes, shapes, colors, and such. They come in all kinds. And so it is with Christians. Yet, let a person spend sufficient time with Jesus, let His grace rather than his own goodness save him and it will show. It will be visible, at least to God.

6. Reuben: Friend with a Donkey

Scripture: Zechariah 9:9-10; Luke 19:29-41

REUBEN SPEAKS

I watched this boy grow up. I intend no disrespect calling him a boy. I always thought of him that way. To me, he was Mary and Joseph's little boy. How well I remember the first time I saw him! He was only a few days old. Mary and Joseph were typical new parents, bursting with pride over their first child. They were spending a few days with us in our home in Bethphage. They had come to Jerusalem to present their newborn child at the temple. However, they were small-town folk from Nazareth and didn't particularly like the city. So they stayed with us a mile or two out in the country. I had known Joseph over the years. We no longer lived near one another, but we kept our friendship alive. He had a well-deserved reputation as an expert craftsman. Frankly, if I knew he was to visit soon, I saved all the repair work that needed doing around the house.

Nazareth and Bethphage were far enough apart that we didn't see much of one another. Yet I saw enough of Mary and Joseph to share their pride in their growing boy. He had a normal childhood. There was the usual joy about the first step and the first word, and the usual consternation the first time he tried to use one of Joseph's hammers—on the furniture, that is! I remember them coming to visit when Jesus was twelve. By then, he was a good-looking boy

55

and full of questions! I had forgotten how many questions a child could ask. Joseph told me that when they went to the temple, he kept the scribes and lawyers busy answering endless questions.

I was shocked to hear of Joseph's death. Jesus was still a very young man when he went to work, taking over his father's trade. It was a heavy responsibility for one so young, but by then there were brothers and sisters who had to be fed and clothed. The next time I saw Jesus he looked so grown up! Joseph had taught him well. He, too, had a way with the hammer and saw. I was pleased he remembered us. Whenever he was near Jerusalem, he made our home one of his stops. As I look back now, I recall the many times on those brief visits we talked about religion. He was quite a thinker. I should have known it would happen with all those questions he asked as a lad. He surprised me with his seriousness about religious matters. He asked me what I thought was happening to Judaism, whether or not the priests in Jerusalem were sincere, if I thought the people were still looking for a Messiah. I'll say this for him, he made me think more about my faith than I had in many years.

I guess it was because of those conversations that I wasn't too startled when I heard he'd given up the carpenter shop and started going around the villages as a teacher of religion. His brothers were old enough to take over the support of the family. I was surprised, though, when I began to hear stories about things he had done. I found it hard to believe Jesus healed the blind, made the lame walk, and things like that. I didn't see him often after he gave up carpentry. I do recall one day he came to our house. We sat and talked for a long, long time. He told me how certain people resented him and how he had had several run-ins with the Pharisees. I could understand it when he explained a few of the things he believed. I'll never forget the end of that conversation when he said, "Reuben, I wonder what it would take to shake our people up, to wake them up to what's happened to their faith. Sometimes I think God expects me to be the person to do just that." Then he went on to say, "I've wondered what would happen if I acted out that old prophecy in Zechariah and rode into Jerusalem proclaiming the Messiah as a lowly prince of peace bringing salvation to the people." I didn't take him too seriously at the time. I thought he had just gotten carried away. But I was wrong, I found out later.

56

One day—it was the day after the sabbath in the week before Passover—two men came to my house. All the roads into Jerusalem were crowded. Pilgrims were arriving from far and wide. There was nothing unusual about unfamiliar faces appearing at the doorway. But there was something strange about the request these two made. They wanted to borrow my donkey. When I asked them why, they said, "Jesus of Nazareth needs it for a while." Well, that was all right. Of course my good friend Jesus could borrow it. So, off they went. I started about my usual round of activities. Maybe an hour or so passed when suddenly I remembered. Like a flash out of heaven, I remembered. I remembered what Jesus had said about acting out Zechariah's prophecy and riding into Jerusalem. *You don't suppose? Oh, no, he wouldn't.* Then I realized that was precisely what he would do.

In five minutes I was on my way to Jerusalem. As I drew near the city gate, I found scraps of palm branches strewn across the path. Ahead was a crowd of shouting, cheering people. I hurried to overtake them. And there he was. Just like he said he'd be, riding on a donkey—my donkey. The crowds were throwing branches and even pieces of their clothing on the ground in front of him. Obviously the people were having the time of their lives. But Jesus? There was no smile on his face. I knew the crowd was missing his point completely. They were simply having a good time. They joined Jesus' friends in shouting the old chant, "Hosanna to the Son of David!" but they didn't mean it. It was just a game, a bit of fun for road-weary pilgrims. His idea had failed. Not even this could shake up the people! When this strange parade approached the temple, I watched Jesus closely. I wondered if anyone else saw the tears come to his eyes. I knew the disappointment behind them. I think I was the only one watching when he slipped off the donkey and disappeared in the mob. The crowd had gone wild, forgetting him in their excitement.

I felt so sorry for Jesus. There were tears in my eyes, too. I noticed my donkey there untended and went over to take its halter. I glanced around but couldn't locate Jesus or his two friends. Slowly I led the donkey out of the city. I could have ridden him, but somehow I didn't want to. All I could think of was Jesus, sitting there in the crowd, utterly disappointed, humiliated, weeping. There flashed through my mind pictures of him as a baby in Mary's arms, as a boy hand in hand with Joseph, as a young man plaguing

57

me with questions. Should I have tried to stop him? Was there anything I could have done? When he first mentioned this plan, should I have told him how foolish I thought it was? I didn't know—I just didn't know. Then I wondered what would happen now. I did know this was Jesus, son of my good friend Joseph. If there was any way possible, I wanted to help.

THE PREACHER REFLECTS

I like this man Reuben. I like anyone who in those last days befriended Jesus. I like him because he helped Jesus by lending his donkey, and because, as he told the story, he wanted to help him even more.

Nevertheless, as everyone else that day, he missed the point. Reuben was right about the people who lined the streets and shouted Hosanna. They obviously missed the point. Yet, in a way, he missed the point, too. He felt sorry for Jesus, having been rejected by the city. It would have been more appropriate to feel sorry for the city having rejected its Lord. So, we appreciate Reuben's sympathy and admire his willingness to help. However, there is a sense in which Jesus needs no help. To the contrary, Jerusalem needed his help then, and we need it now.

JESUS NEEDS NO HELP

He does seem rather pitiful riding into Jerusalem on a donkey. Traditionally we call the events of that day the triumphal entry. It was an entry all right. Jesus did go into Jerusalem. But in what sense was it a triumph? In no sense that immediately meets the eye. Triumph over what? Jerusalem? Surely not. The city was unchanged on Monday. Rome? Surely not. The whole thing was unnoticed. His enemies? Surely not. They plotted while he paraded. So he does look rather pitiful and helpless riding along on a donkey. Yet to see it that way is to misunderstand the drama in the event.

Today we are accustomed to seeing candidates for public office parade through our streets. They round up several late model automobiles, decorate them with red, white, and blue bunting, attach the appropriate party slogans, and ride off to seek support. They are candidates for an office, seeking the necessary public support and vote to attain that office. Perhaps, at first glance, what Jesus did back there in the streets of Jerusalem seems similar to

58

that. Here was a man seeking public support, a candidate to be Messiah and Lord. Here was a man begging the public to get behind him and make him Lord. Then, when people did not get behind him, when they made the whole thing into a lark, he wept for lack of support. No—that was not it at all. This was no candidate for the office of Lord. This was the Lord. This was no pretender to a throne. This was the King himself. Jesus was not riding through the streets of Jerusalem saying, "Come help me become Lord. I need your support and vote." He was riding through the streets of Jerusalem as Lord and King. He did not need the help of that crowd to become Lord. He does not need our help today to become King. He is Lord of all men. God has made him so. He is the King of life. God has made him so. Jesus is not dependent on us for his reign and authority. He does not beg us to give him authority to become Lord. We do not make him Lord by our response. He is Lord and does not need our help to become Lord. Peter, in his sermon at Pentecost, said, "God has made him both Lord and Christ, this Jesus . . ." (Acts 2:36).

In recent years great stress has been placed upon seeing Jesus as the Suffering Servant. I understand that. I appreciate Jesus as the servant for whom no task is too menial, no service too mundane. Nevertheless, that servant image should not obscure his Lordship. Too often Jesus is pictured as a kindly man who wandered about Palestine begging people to join up with him, begging them to endorse his candidacy. Unfortunately only a handful responded, perhaps no more than a dozen. Even they fell away when needed most. We pity this poor, friendless beggar whose call for help and helpers went unheard and unheeded. Nonsense! Jesus did not beg for followers to help him become something. He announced the truth and invited men to share in it. As he sat there astride the donkey, he wept not for himself. He wept not out of self-pity, nor for lack of support. He wept for the city. He had not asked Jerusalem to make him Lord. He needed no help for that. He had asked Jerusalem to share in the fruits of his Lordship. Let no man weep for poor Jesus lacking support. Let him weep for Jerusalem refusing its Lord. Shame on the church if it pussyfoots around the world, half apologetically saying, "Come on. Give Jesus a hand. He wants to be Lord. He ought to be Lord. But he can't make the grade until everyone votes for him." He is Lord! He needs no help for that. God has made him Lord.

59

WE NEED HIS HELP

Jerusalem needed Jesus. The city needed its Lord, and we need the Lord Jesus, too. I don't know what images those words conjure up for you. They express some honest feelings of mine. We need Jesus. The world is in a sad state of affairs and so is the nation. We are frightened and apprehensive, and well we should be. However, we shouldn't be surprised. If Jesus is Lord, then that means life works the way he said it works. When we try to work it any other way, to use the bluntest language I know, all hell breaks loose. That is precisely what has happened. Hell has broken loose in the world because in a world where life works the Jesus way, men have stubbornly tried to make it work some other way and that's what is bound to happen. When men refuse to love one another, when nations lift up swords against one another, the world will shake and nations will tremble. Because Jesus is Lord, life works his way. We work it his way, or else.

Remember the hymn, "I need Jesus, my need I now confess. . ."? In a way, that's what this old world is saying with all of its problems and difficulties. From Washington to Hanoi to Saigon, from Watergate to London, from ghetto to suburb, we need Jesus. The old world may not verbalize that, but the nonverbal communication of its hellish problems makes the message clear enough: We need Jesus. He needs no help in becoming Lord. We need his help in trying to live in this world.

The challenge of the gospel is not that Christ can't get along without us. He can get along without us. He doesn't need us to make him Lord. But wonder of wonders, he is not willing to get along without us. He may not need us, but he wants us. Not willing to get along without us, he shares the glories of his kingdom and Lordship with us. He rode into the city, not to get something, but to give something, not to get help, but to give help, not to attain Lordship, but to share it. This Jesus needs no help. True, but this world needs his help and so do I.

There is a story of a cowboy who heard about Jesus and the donkey and the city. Apparently he had never heard of the incident before. When the telling was over, he said of Jesus, "What wonderful hands he must have had!" When asked how he had reached that conclusion, he pointed out that for a man to take an untrained donkey who had never been ridden and guide him through a shrieking mob, he would have to have wonderful hands.[1] Jesus needed no help in managing the donkey or in becoming Lord. I need help. If I let his wonderful hands get hold of "mulish" me, he can manage me into full life where I'll enjoy the fruits of his Lordship.

[1] Leslie S. Weatherhead, *His Life and Ours* (Nashville: Abingdon Press, 1933), p. 209-210.

7. Joseph: Man with a Tomb

Scripture: John 19:38-42

JOSEPH SPEAKS

Let me set things straight right away. I am no hero. I want no praise. I'm not proud of what I did. I'm glad I buried Jesus in my tomb, but there are other things for which I'm sorry. I tell you my story not to defend myself but because telling it somehow makes me feel better.

Actually I was a small-town boy. I grew up in a little village in the hills north of Jerusalem—Arimathea. I inherited a small business which my father had started. When he died, I decided to move the business to Jerusalem. Almost overnight, life changed from penny-pinching to plenty. My wife, Martha, and I moved into a larger home. Slowly, we were accepted in the circles of influential people. I would be less than honest if I said we didn't enjoy this life. We did, and it was climaxed by my election to the Sanhedrin. Occasionally, as I sat in the sessions of the Sanhedrin, listened to the learned discussions and cast my vote on certain issues, I smiled—small-town Joseph had done very well in the big city!

One of my closest friends in Jerusalem was a man named Nicodemus. Like me he was a Pharisee and a member of the Sanhedrin. Our families were together often. We thoroughly enjoyed one another's company. He was not as rich as I; I was not

63

as religious as he. I imagine I was elected to the Sanhedrin because of my prosperity and Nicodemus because of his piety. It was our friendship and his faith that first brought me into contact with Jesus of Nazareth. Nicodemus had heard him teach and preach. Several times I went with him to hear Jesus. From the very beginning, I was attracted to Him. Much of what Jesus said seemed to make plain, good sense. He talked language I could understand. Many of my friends in the Sanhedrin were far over my head, but this man used words I knew and told stories I understood. Maybe it was a case of one small-town man talking to another. Nicodemus and I never told anyone else about these gatherings we attended. We knew other members of the Sanhedrin were worried about the growing popularity of Jesus—and they had good reason to be worried. Some of what he said was hard on the temple system. A few of the followers of Jesus discovered who we were. They kept our secret, but they argued with us. They said it would be a great help to Jesus if two people of our standing and prominence would come out publicly in his favor. We declined and chose to remain as anonymous friends rather than followers.

Then came the fateful night. I was sound asleep when one of the servants awakened me. A messenger had come from Caiaphas bringing word there was to be an emergency session of the Sanhedrin immediately. Members were to gather at the high priest's house at once. This was most unusual. I hadn't been in the Sanhedrin long, but I had never heard of meetings in the middle of the night. As I made my way along the darkened streets, I wondered what could be this important. I soon found out. When I was ushered into the room where the others were gathering, there was Jesus, bound like a prisoner. To say I was shocked would be an understatement. I looked for Nicodemus, made my way over to him, and sat down beside him. Shortly thereafter, the proceedings began. "Proceedings" is too nice a word for what happened—"farce" would be a better word. It was called a trial, but if that was justice, I want no justice for myself.

They were trying Jesus. Several witnesses appeared, saying things Nicodemus and I simply did not believe. But the rest of the Sanhedrin believed them. I can't explain what happened that night. These were dignified men normally, very sophisticated, most restrained, and generally fair. But not that night! Jesus didn't have a chance, not a chance. Several times I wanted to jump up and

64

protest, but I seemed glued to my chair. Once or twice, when Jesus looked over the council, his eyes paused on mine and I melted. I knew he recognized me. I felt he was pleading with me. Finally the matter came to a vote. Caiaphas put it simply, "All those who favor the conviction of this man, vote yea." Every member but Nicodemus and I shouted yea. Caiaphas noticed our silence, stared angrily at us and said, "Anyone opposing this conviction, say no." I waited for Nicodemus to speak. I guess he waited for me. Neither of us spoke. The silence thundered in my ears. Then Caiaphas shouted, "Jesus of Nazareth, you stand convicted. We shall seek Pilate's order for your execution."

Well, they got Pilate's order. By noon the next day, Jesus was on the cross. Members of the Sanhedrin were expected to be present. I didn't want to go, but I went. I watched while he slowly died. And they didn't just let him die. He was laughed at, cursed, ridiculed. It all seemed cruel and senseless to me. By three in the afternoon, it was over. I made my way home.

I went directly to my room. I asked Martha to leave me alone for a while. I wanted to think by myself. I wonder how many people have ever had the feeling I had that afternoon. I helped to kill that man! No matter how I tried to reason my way out of it, his blood was on my hands. His death was on my conscience. And the horrible thing about it all was that I knew him. I don't know how long I'd been there in my room, but an idea began to form in my mind. I had been afraid to help Jesus earlier, but maybe there was something I could do now. I had a new tomb just outside the city wall. That was another of those things that went with having money. I got the idea that perhaps I could secure the body of Jesus and bury it in my tomb. Maybe that would make up for things somehow. I told Martha where I was going and went to the house of Nicodemus. I found him in a mood like mine. When I told him what I was thinking about, he cautioned me, "Joseph, it will be the end of you. You can't do it in secret. You'll have to go ask Pilate for the body. They'll throw you off the Sanhedrin and make a public spectacle of you." I could scarcely believe my own words when I heard myself saying, "I don't care what it costs me. I'm going to do it." Nicodemus was quiet for a few minutes and then said, "I won't go with you, Joseph, but if you've got the courage to go to Pilate, I'll help you bury him."

I went to Pilate. I wasn't very brave. I was shaking all over. Pilate

65

said, "Joseph, you're a fool, an absolute fool. Caiaphas will have your hide." He paused, and then went on, "I understand how you feel. Claudia and I have been upset by this whole thing, but you'll be damned, Joseph." I persisted—how, I don't know, but I did. Finally Pilate checked with the soldiers to make sure Jesus was in fact dead. He wrote out a permit and handed it to me saying, "Good-bye, Joseph, and I do mean good-bye."

Nicodemus went with me to get the body. We wrapped it in a linen shroud. I don't think we said a single word to one another as we carried the body to my tomb. When we arrived at the spot, we laid Jesus down. We stood there for awhile, each of us with his own thoughts. Then, Nicodemus tugged at my sleeve and we turned away. Together we rolled the stone over the opening. As we walked home, we were still silent. I thought about those times Jesus looked at me during the trial, looked at me as if pleading with me. Then I thought about what Nicodemus and I had just done, and what it would cost us. I didn't care about that. I was glad that we had done it, whatever the cost. I put my arm around my friend's shoulders and said, "I wish he knew!"

THE PREACHER REFLECTS

We can understand Joseph's wish for Jesus to know. Of course he wanted him to know that he stepped forward, took all the risks involved, and gave his body a decent burial. Well, he does know. That's one of the things that Easter teaches us. Jesus is not gone. He is not dead and gone. He is alive. He is here and alive. So of course he knows what any man does or doesn't do. Joseph can rest assured that Jesus knows what he did.

There are those who think Joseph did not do enough. They accuse him of doing too little too late. Many a preacher has been exceedingly harsh with Joseph. He has been called the secret disciple, and that's not meant as a compliment. True, he did keep his discipleship a secret. Yet, how many of us would reveal our discipleship if it would cost us as much as it probably cost him? He has been called the silent disciple and that's not meant as a compliment either. True, he did not speak up to defend Jesus in the Sanhedrin. Yet, how many of us with similar odds against us would find words to speak?

Before judging Joseph, one ought to take into account when he did what he did. When he finally acted, and acted with great

66

courage, it was before Easter, not after. Think for a moment what that means. We live on this side of Easter. We have the benefit of the resurrection as a confirmation of this man's life and teachings. We have the benefit of two thousand years of man's experience with the risen, living Lord. But Joseph had none of that. All he had was a memory. As far as he knew, it was all over. Jesus was dead and gone—that was that! Yet, Joseph with that limited perspective did what he did. He contaminated his tomb with the body of an executed criminal. It could never be used for anyone else. He surrendered his coveted position on the powerful Sanhedrin. He jeopardized his business future and risked his life. And all of that for a dead man. I find that I can't be too harsh on Joseph. I know more, much more, than he did about this Jesus. But I must ask, "Have I done more or less than he did for Jesus? I may not be a secret or a silent disciple as he was, but what by way of comparison has my obvious discipleship cost me?" I cannot condemn Joseph. I honor him.

Actually, I both praise and pity Joseph. Let me try to explain those feelings. Easter is sometimes referred to as the third day. Jesus rose from the dead on the third day. Joseph did his burying before that day. I think there are second-day disciples and third-day disciples. One kind lives on the other side of Easter, and one kind lives on this side of Easter. Joseph, I believe, was a second-day disciple, and like all second-day disciples, he is to be praised and pitied. He is to be praised because he was a disciple, and pitied because he lived on the wrong side of Easter. It is better to be a third-day disciple. Let us ponder over that matter. Which are we, second- or third-day disciples? In terms of time, of course we live on this side of Easter. However, it is possible in terms of faith (or the lack of it) to live on the other side.

SECOND-DAY DISCIPLES

That second day must have been a dreadful one. Jesus, as we put it, had been laid to rest. Nicodemus had provided more than enough spices, and Joseph had provided a choice burial plot. He had a fine burying, as some would say, but he was dead. The people he had healed were still healed. The principles by which he had lived were still right and true. The two great commandments— love of God and love of neighbor—were still in force. Nothing he had revealed had been revoked. But he was dead. Love was still

67

love. Goodness was still goodness. Sacrifice was still sacrifice. One could still go on living, loving, sacrificing. But he was dead. A second-day disciple has nothing but memories. Those memories are not to be minimized. The memory of Christ's strength has kept many a man strong; the memory of his courage has kept many a man courageous; the memory of his tenderness has kept many a man tender; the memory of his righteousness has kept many a man righteous. But they are just memories. For Joseph, those memories were strong enough to prompt him to risk everything, and for that he is to be praised. However, he is to be pitied too. Apparently, he never did move beyond Saturday, the second day, in his experience. Though it was his tomb, and it all took place on his property, he has no role in the Easter drama. Further, though providing this burial branded him unmistakably as a disciple, he plays no known role in the subsequent development of the Christian community. One can only conclude that Joseph buried Jesus and lived with his memories. He may have lived nobly, faithfully, even sacrificially, but it must have been on that other side of Easter. He lived with the memory of a dead Jesus rather than with the presence of the living Lord. He is to be praised and pitied. So are all those for whom the third day never dawns.

THIRD-DAY DISCIPLES

If second-day disciples are to be praised and pitied, third-day disciples are to be praised and envied. They have more than a memory to recall; they have a person to call upon. Even if the third day had never dawned, even without Easter, Christ's teachings were true. His principles were valid and practicable. However, third-day disciples have more than principles; they have a presence. They have more than objective truth; they have a living Lord.

Years ago, we were taking a Sunday afternoon ride through the back roads of Vermont. Much to our delight we came upon a covered bridge. We stopped and took the usual pictures. Then we noticed a sign. It wasn't large and I don't recall its exact wording. It informed us that this bridge had been preserved by an official-sounding organization by the name of The Society for the Preservation and Restoration of Covered Bridges. Some may think that's a good description of the disciple band then and now: a

68

society for the preservation of something out of the past. They understand it as a society to preserve the memory of a good man, once living, now dead. That is second-day discipleship on which the third day's sun has never shone. The second-day disciple may keep the memory of his Lord alive, but the third-day disciple is kept alive by his Lord.

The second-day disciple says he is remembered.

The third-day disciple says he is risen.

The second-day disciple sees Jesus put to rest.

The third-day disciple sees him come to life.

The second-day disciple performs an office for the dead.

The third-day disciple performs a service for the living.

The second-day disciple is a burial Christian with a lovely memory.

The third-day disciple is a resurrection Christian with a lively Lord.

They are both disciples and both are praiseworthy. However, one is to be pitied, and the other envied.

We are in Joseph's debt. He did for Jesus what no one else would do. He put him in his tomb. We hope he came at last to put him in his heart.

A certain Mr. Hall once visited the Holy Land. He planned to attend the traditional sunrise service on Easter morning. He had hired a guide, a Christian Arab. He spent a restless night waiting for the dawn to come. At one point he turned to the guide and asked, "Will this night never pass?" Said the guide, "Never fear, my friend. The day will come. You can't hold back the dawn."[1]

Ah, but you can! You can live on the other side of Easter, a second-day disciple with just a memory. Or you can let the sun come up and live on this side of Easter, a third-day disciple with a living Lord.

[1] Leslie D. Weatherhead, *Key Next Door* (Nashville: Abingdon Press, 1959), p. 170.

69

Part Two
Among Those Listening

Introduction

The seven last words of Jesus have been cherished by twenty centuries of Christians. The cross occasionally has been described as his finest pulpit. Each Lenten season we listen to the seven words from the cross, eager to hear what truth they have to share. We have heard them many times and have listened as preachers have strained for fresh interpretations. Perhaps we forget how those seven words initially were heard and received.

In the materials that follow, an attempt is made to hear the seven last words as they were first heard. Gathered around the foot of that cross were individuals of considerable variety. A few were sympathizers—friends, family, and followers who were brought there by loyalty or love. A few were bystanders—folks who just happened to be around and followed the excitement out to the hill. A few were enemies—men of power who judged Jesus dangerous. A few were functionaries—soldiers and such with a job to do. These were the people who were among the multitude and were listening that day.

Seven persons scattered throughout that multitude are interviewed in the following pages. There is New Testament testimony to the presence of most of them, and involvement in the scene seems a reasonable assumption for the rest. Each of these persons is presented as having had some unique reason for hearing and

71

remembering one of the seven words. His or her past or present experience with Christ made the personal appropriation of that particular word likely.

There is a similar pattern in all of the presentations provided. First, the passages of Scripture which contain the word from the cross and the reference to the character are suggested for reading. That reading of the word may be followed by an anthem which contains the same word. The music not only enriches the sermonizing but gives the choir a feeling of participation in the proclamation. Second, the preacher begins an introduction in which he presents both the word and the individual. As that introduction draws to a conclusion, the character approaches the chancel where he will be interviewed. This character should be costumed and may move down an aisle from the rear of the church. When he arrives at the chancel, the preacher should move from behind the pulpit or lectern to meet him and then proceed immediately with the interview. Both preacher and character should memorize the interview and should rehearse it as long as required to give the appearance of spontaneity. The use of a hand microphone is a near necessity and practice with it a requirement. When the interview is completed, the third phase of interpretation begins. For this, the preacher returns to his pulpit as the character exits. Attention to lighting may increase the dramatic effect. Distracting and unnecessary motion and/or furniture rearrangement should be minimal.

The preacher will note that the content contains problems of timing and knowledge. In asking questions, he occasionally appears ignorant of facts which everyone present is aware he knows. He is talking to people who have long since died and who, in some cases, did move on subsequently to different faith positions. Experience indicates that congregations are able to use their imaginations and not be troubled by these inconsistencies. It is possible, of course, for a third person to conduct the interview. However, the preacher is by far the best choice.

Costuming of the characters will add immeasurably to the drama of the interview. Most large cities have rental companies where good quality costumes can be secured, and they are worth the modest cost. Many churches have sizable wardrobes available for loan. Authenticity is the goal.

72

"Father, forgive them. . . ."

8. A Woman Made New
Scripture: Luke 23:33-34

INTRODUCTION

Mary Magdalene was present at the crucifixion. We can assume she heard Jesus say, "Father, forgive them; for they know not what they do." The Gospel According to John vouches for her presence saying, "Standing by the cross of Jesus were his mother, and his mother's sister . . . and Mary Magdalene" (John 19:25). It was right that she should be there. She had been one of his most faithful followers throughout the last months of his life.

It all began when Christ healed her. The New Testament says Jesus cast seven demons out of her. Small wonder she was devoted to him. Actually, Mary has been a much maligned person. She has been accused of every conceivable vice and pictured as little better than a common prostitute. It may be surprising to learn there is little justification for this in the Bible. Tradition has identified her with the bold woman in Luke's Gospel who washed Jesus' feet dried them with her hair, and anointed them with fine perfume. Yet there is no real support for such identification because the woman remains unnamed in Luke's text (Luke 7:36:50). She may owe some of her unfortunate reputation to her hometown. She came from Magdala, hence she was called Magdalene. Magdala was a wicked city and infamous as a mecca for vice and immorality. However, we have no reason to suspect that Mary herself was party

73

to any of that. We do know she was quite well-to-do. She evidently contributed substantial amounts to keep the Jesus movement going. She was an impulsive sort, perhaps rather emotional. She played the same role among the women as Peter did among the men. She was one of the first to arrive at the tomb on Easter morning and may have been the very first to whom the risen Christ appeared. Jesus had made a new woman out of her—literally. And she loved him for it. So this Mary, Mary Magdalene, was among those present that day.

INTERVIEW

PREACHER: Mary, how did you happen to be there? Why were you there?

MARY: I couldn't stay away. I had to be there!

PREACHER: What do you mean you had to be there?

MARY: Well, someone had to be there. Most of the disciples already had left the city. The other followers were afraid to be there. I couldn't leave him. I didn't think he should have to suffer like that—all alone out there without any friends.

PREACHER: So there weren't many of his friends there?

MARY: No, only a handful—three or four maybe.

PREACHER: How did you feel? Were you frightened?

MARY: I was too upset to be frightened. I couldn't believe what was going on. I still shudder every time I think about it.

PREACHER: It must have been a sad day for you.

MARY: Sad, yes. But to be perfectly honest with you, I was mad, too. It was all so wrong—so stupid!

PREACHER: You mean you don't think he got a fair trial?

MARY: Oh, I don't know much about the trial. I'm no lawyer and I don't pretend to understand all that. Yet here was the kindest, most loving person who ever lived, and look what they did to him! They made fun of him. They spat on him. They cursed him. They treated him like the scum of the earth, a common criminal.

PREACHER: Then you wouldn't call him a criminal?

MARY: Criminal? What crime had he committed? Is it a crime to help people? Is it wrong to teach men how to live a better life? Is it against the law to help people?

PREACHER: Then you would say he didn't mean any harm?

MARY: Harm? Of course not. He wouldn't harm a soul. He loved

74

everybody. He wanted to help all people. Look at me! I was nothing, no good to myself or anybody else. Look what he did to me! I'm a decent, healthy, whole person all because of Jesus.

PREACHER: I can see he meant a lot to you.

MARY: He meant everything to me. As far as I'm concerned, he was the finest person who ever lived on earth.

PREACHER: Then what went wrong? Why did these other people want to get rid of him?

MARY: Because they were stupid, that's why!

PREACHER: Stupid? That's a rather strong word. You know you're talking about the leaders of your own people?

MARY: I know it's a strong word, but that's the way I feel. They may have been important people, but that time they were stupid. Here was a man who meant no one any harm, who did nothing but good, and they had him killed. That's stupid. They didn't know what they were doing!

PREACHER: So you were mad. Did you and the other followers consider trying to do something, like getting revenge?

MARY: How could we?

PREACHER: I don't know. You mean there were too few of you to do anything like that?

MARY: No. I mean, how could we when Jesus said what he said?

PREACHER: Why? What did he say?

MARY: There he was, hanging on a cross, looking down on all those people who wanted him out of the way and what did he say? "Father, forgive them; for they know not what they do."

PREACHER: Are you sure that's what he said?

MARY: Of course, I'm sure. I heard him. And I'm just as certain that they did not know what they were doing!

INTERPRETATION

That first word of forgiveness has new meaning for me when I listen to it through the ears of Mary. "Father, forgive them, for they know not what they do!" I always have heard the forgiveness there. Here is this amazingly magnanimous Jesus. He hangs there on a cross, suffering excruciating pain, and he worries about the people who have put him there. That's going the second mile, turning the other cheek, and returning good for evil all wrapped up in one grand, unbelievable act of forgiving love. That forgiveness is there and I've heard it. However, Mary helps me to hear something else.

75

When I listen to that word through her ears, I hear more than loving forgiveness. I hear stern judgment as well. Jesus says simply and bluntly that the people who did this thing to him did not know what they were doing. That's judgment. He accuses his enemies of not knowing what they were doing.

The interesting thing is that they seemed to know precisely what they were doing. That is what most disturbs us about all of this experience. The whole thing from betrayal to trial to execution seemed so cold and calculating. Everyone played his part with practiced precision. Pilate knew what he was doing—he was an expert at both humiliation and evasion. Caiaphas knew what he was doing—anyone who upset things at the temple should be punished properly. The soldiers knew what they were doing—they were masters at the art of cruelty and had developed sinister innovations to add to the pain. The bystanders knew what they were doing—they provided the deserved ridicule for such a foolish pretender. They all knew what they were doing. Yet they didn't know! They didn't know that this was the Christ, the son of God, and what they did was put him on a cross to prove that he wasn't. They refused to know him as the Christ and erected a cross to prove the rightness of their refusal.

THEY KNOW NOT WHAT THEY DO

It was rather hard to believe. It was no easy thing to believe that this humble carpenter of Nazareth was the Son of God. Of course, he had some unique powers and keen insights. His healings were beyond dispute; his ethical principles above reproach. Yet, nothing about him commended him to them as the long-awaited Messiah. How could a man who spent his time with society's outcasts, ate with publicans and sinners defended prostitutes, disregarded the sacred sabbath law, and finally disrupted the temple with a violent attack on the money changers be the Son of God? The whole idea was preposterous, and the cross would prove it. The cross was an effective instrument for doing that. It destroyed a man and all his dreams and claims. The public scandal of the execution would put an end to all popular expectations.

We're told that a picture found scribbled on a Roman wall in the first half of the first century depicted a man bowing before a cross. On the cross was the figure of a man, but it was a man with an ass's head. Underneath was scrawled, "Alex. [sic] the Jew worships his

76

God."[1] A cross was for an ass, not a Son of God. Paul said, "We preach Christ crucified, unto the Jews a stumblingblock, and unto the Greeks foolishness" (1 Corinthians 1:23, KJV). One interpreter says that the word "foolishness" isn't strong enough. The word is more like our word "obscenity."[2] Cicero said, "It is a word with which no Roman gentleman would soil his lips."[3] To speak of Christ crucified was to use a contradiction in terms. If Christ, then not crucified. If crucified, then not Christ.

They refused to know this man as the Christ. They erected a cross to prove the rightness of their refusal. They knew not what they did: what they knew not was that he was the Christ; what they did was put up a cross. "Father, forgive them, for they know not what they do."

WE DO NOT WHAT WE KNOW

So much for the ancient crowd that gathered there and the special word of judgment and forgiveness spoken to them. What about us? What about the crowds who gather at the foot of the cross today? Is there a special word of judgment and forgiveness for us? I think so—not because we know not what we do, but because we do not what we know. We know that the man there on the central cross was the Christ, the Son of God. What we do not is take up his cross and follow him. We do not what we know. What we know is that this is the Christ; what we do not is take up his cross.

At one point in his ministry, Jesus was preparing the disciples for the cross. He told them he would be abused and crucified. Peter protested: "Not you, Lord, nothing like that for you!" Jesus listened to Peter's protest but told him in no uncertain terms he was mistaken. Then he went on immediately to say: "If any man would come after me, let him deny himself and take up his cross and follow me" (Matthew 16:24). If we know him as the Christ, we ought to take up the cross. However, some of us stand at the foot of the cross, hear his words of forgiveness, and appropriate them to our salvation. Yet we turn a deaf ear when he dares to suggest that those who would follow him must take up a cross also. Just so, we do not what we know. The cross was something wonderful done

[1] Leslie D. Weatherhead, *That Immortal Sea* (Nashville: Abingdon Press, 1953), p. 180—comments in a footnote.
[2] *Ibid.*
[3] *Ibid.*

77

for us, but it was something demanded of us too. Someone has written, "We want the Christ but not His cross; we want the church, but not the discipline it requires in terms of sacrifice of time, talent, and life. We want its worship, but not on a rainy morning. . . . We want the teaching of the church for our children, but only if we do not oversleep, or the grass is not too high."[4] So we do not what we know.

In one of Yeats's plays there is a scene in a country cottage in Ireland. The family sits together in the firelight of the kitchen. "On the wall there hangs a black wooden crucifix. There is a knock at the door, and when it is opened, in comes a fairy girl, dressed in green, singing a merry song. . . . Suddenly her eyes fall upon the crucifix, and she stops her singing and hides her face, and cries out: 'Take down that ugly black thing.'"[5] The cross was an ugly black thing. How we try to avoid it as that! We try to camouflage it. We dangle it as an ornamental trinket about our necks, wear it as a lapel pin, use it indiscriminately as a decorative design. A confectioner advertised chocolate-covered crosses for Easter. We will do almost anything with the cross, except take it up and bear it. We will not do what we know. Yet, it was a cross-centered faith that the New Testament proclaimed and it is only such a faith that is worth proclaiming today.

Pink-pill Christianity may appeal to semi-neurotics, but the only Christianity capable of capturing the imagination and loyalty of intelligent, red-blooded men is a Christianity with the Cross at its heart and centre. What was it indeed that sent the apostles out in the face of bitter and bloody persecution to turn a hostile, pagan world upside down; that sent Paul on his journeys and took martyrs into the Roman Colosseum; that inspired the Reformers and sent missionaries to the far corners of the earth? Not a popular preacher telling them to relax, but a lonely man treading the dark road to Calvary, and saying to a handful of disciples, "If any man would come after me, let him deny himself and take up his cross and follow me."[6]

We know that is what we ought to do.

An old novel has the title *The Trampled Cross*. It was the story of a British soldier who fell into the hands of the Arabs. They had

[4] Robert F. Jones, *Seven Words to the Cross* (Richmond: John Knox Press, 1961), p. 19.

[5] Referred to in Donald M. Baillie, *Out of Nazareth* (New York: Charles Scribner's Sons, 1958), p. 62.

[6] A. Leonard Griffith, *Beneath the Cross of Jesus* (Nashville: Abingdon Press, 1961), p. 64.

been fighting one another in the desert. The Arabs were about to kill the Britisher when they thought of an amusing trick. The Arab chieftain took two sticks and placed them on the ground before the soldier, forming a cross. Said he, "There is the symbol of your faith. Trample on it, and we shall let you go free."[7] We do trample on it—not literally, but figuratively. We trample on it by neglecting it, ignoring it, decorating it, doing everything with it but taking it up. We know this man is the Christ. How dare we not take up his cross and follow him?

So, I can stand there at the cross with Mary Magdalene and ponder the stupidity of those who didn't know what they were doing, and the stupidity of us who aren't doing what we know. This first word from the cross becomes two:

"Father, forgive them, for they know not what they do."

"Father, forgive us, for we do not what we know."

[7] *Ibid.*, p. 67.

"Today you will be with me. . . ."

9. A Rebel Let Loose

Scripture: Matthew 27:15-18; 20-23; Luke 23:39-43

INTRODUCTION

Barabbas surely was there. How could he have stayed away? That man on the central cross had literally taken his place there. Those men on the other two crosses undoubtedly were friends of his. Barabbas had been in prison, but he was not a common thief. There was nothing common about him. The name Barabbas means (Bar) son (abbas) of a Father. That may indicate that he was a son of one of the Fathers. He may very well have been a son of one of the nation's leaders, or one of the teachers of the Jewish law. So there was nothing common about him, and his crime was not common thievery. He was called a robber, but the word thus translated means something other than purse snatcher or the like. It denotes a revolutionary. Thus we can picture Barabbas brought up among the religious aristocracy, taught Jewish tradition, and nurtured by refined parents. Then he became a rebel. We can imagine him arguing long hours with his father. Perhaps the father maintained that the only hope for Israel was patiently to tolerate the hated Romans, while the son passionately insisted that the enemy should be destroyed. Sooner or later that revolutionary passion led to rebellious action and Barabbas was imprisoned.

A few scholars are confident that he had another name, the given name of Jesus. They suggest that on that fateful Friday, Barabbas

81

was dragged out of his prison cell into Pilate's court. There he stood on one side of Pilate; the carpenter from Nazareth on the other. Pilate said to the people, "Which Jesus shall I set free? Jesus called Barabbas or Jesus called Christ?" And the crowd chose Barabbas for freedom and the carpenter for crucifixion. Two strong men exchanged places. They were both named Jesus, both leaders of other men, both passionately committed to the establishment of a kingdom. They were similar in some ways, yet very, very different from each other. This Barabbas, Jesus Barabbas, was present that day.

INTERVIEW

PREACHER: Barabbas, why were you there?

BARABBAS: Well, where would you expect me to be? That's where all the excitement was!

PREACHER: I thought maybe you'd had enough excitement for one day.

BARABBAS: I'd had plenty I'll tell you—there's no way to describe how it felt to walk out through those prison doors.

PREACHER: Did you think all along that you might get out?

BARABBAS: Not a chance! I already could feel those nails in my hands—and then, just like that, I was free.

PREACHER: Had you known anything about this other Jesus?

BARABBAS: Not much. That's one of the reasons I wanted to be there on the hill. I was curious about him.

PREACHER: Curious?

BARABBAS: Sure—wouldn't you be curious about somebody who was executed instead of you?

PREACHER: Yes, I'm certain I would. You must have felt odd standing there watching him die.

BARABBAS: Very odd! I don't know what I expected, but he sure wasn't anything like I thought he'd be.

PREACHER: How do you mean?

BARABBAS: I'm no angel, and if the people preferred to have him out of the way rather than me, I guess I thought he had to be a real bad character.

PREACHER: Then when you saw him he didn't seem like that?

BARABBAS: Not really. I've been around a lot and seen all kinds of people, but I never saw one quite like him.

PREACHER: How was he different?

BARABBAS: I don't know how to describe it—but people just couldn't seem to keep from looking at him. He obviously was the center of attention. Nobody even noticed anyone else who was there.

PREACHER: Why? Was he yelling, or screaming, or creating a stir?

BARABBAS: No, it wasn't that kind of thing. Actually, he seemed quite calm. But there was something sort of strange about him. Some people were cursing him and others were weeping for him. Some spat on him and others tried to comfort him. He just seemed like the kind of person you couldn't ignore. The other two guys were completely ignored.

PREACHER: I suspect you didn't ignore them.

BARABBAS: No—they had been friends of mine. We spent a lot of time in prison together. I was sorry they weren't set free too, but their luck ran out. I was surprised though, at what happened to them.

PREACHER: Why, what did happen?

BARABBAS: Well, they were like everybody else. They couldn't keep their eyes off this other Jesus. As a matter of fact they got to arguing with one another about him. There they were dying— and arguing about this Jesus on the other cross!

PREACHER: What was there to argue about?

BARABBAS: Well, Gesmas was making fun of Jesus, telling him to work a miracle and set them all free; and Dismas was telling Gesmas to shut up and listen to what the man had to say. Not even those two rebels could ignore him, or agree on him either!

PREACHER: Do you recall anything in particular that was said, anything that made an impression on you?

BARABBAS: Well, I did hear this Jesus promise Dismas a place in paradise. I'll be honest. I can't feature Dismas in any place called paradise.

PREACHER: How do you explain the way your friends reacted to him, or got involved with him there?

BARABBAS: I can't. Apparently he was a man that made you decide for him or against him.

PREACHER: In that case, how did you decide? You were there!

BARABBAS: I was afraid you'd ask me that. I don't know that I have decided yet. But I know I've got to—and I'll tell you this: it does something to you when a man dies for you.

INTERPRETATION

Barabbas, as presented here, exhibited considerable insight. He was right in the way he sized up this other Jesus. He was the kind of person who demanded decision. People who met him seemed compelled to decide for him or against him. Even those two friends of Barabbas discovered that to be true. One would think that two men dying a horrible death by crucifixion would have enough to think about and would be preoccupied with their own suffering. But even they could not ignore Jesus. Even they had to decide about him. They could not ignore him. One decided for him; the other against him.

The writers of the New Testament were impressed with this quality of Jesus. They called it the authority of Jesus and described him "as one who had authority" (Matthew 7:29). They were mystified about the source of that authority. They didn't know where he got it or why. Yet he obviously had it. There was something authoritative and commanding about him. He was certain about himself and what he was doing—certain even when on a cross.

We risk losing sight of that side of Jesus. We run that risk especially when we focus on the cross and the events leading up to it. We see him as despised and rejected of men, wounded and bruised. We think of him as one who bowed his head and calmly took the misuse and abuse heaped upon him. It's a sad and pitiful picture. Yet, that picture doesn't do complete justice to Jesus. There was something commanding and authoritative about him right up to the last. He boldly made a shambles of the temple courtyard, turning over the tables and scattering the coins. He confidently walked out to meet his captors in Gethsemane. He confronted Pilate and Herod and they immediately had a bad case of the jitters, nervously shuttling him back and forth. He bravely refused a sedative in the midst of his suffering. He openly accused his enemies of tragic stupidity—of not knowing what they were doing. True, he was a captive. True, he was bound. True, he was ridiculed and roughed up by the soldiers. True, he was a victim. But it seemed to some that even in all of that he was in charge. That Jesus on the cross was an authoritative, commanding man. He was a man sure of himself and certain of his position. That is what Barabbas sensed about him and what the two thieves experienced in his presence.

84

DECIDING HE IS RIGHT

Dismas, as tradition has called the repentant thief, said, "Jesus, remember me when you come in your kingly power." That's a rather remarkable request—remarkable on two counts. It is remarkable in the way Dismas addressed Jesus and remarkable in what he asked. Dismas addressed Jesus simply as "Jesus." That is the only place in the entire New Testament where another person in direct address says simply "Jesus." In all other places a title is added. Even when this verse appears in the King James Version, the title "Lord" is used. But that must have been force of habit on the part of the translator. In the New Testament Greek there is nothing but the simple name "Jesus." Thus, Dismas addressed Jesus with a familiarity unknown throughout the balance of the Gospels. That has prompted interpreters to suspect that Jesus and Dismas were longtime friends. Perhaps they grew up together and were chums in the neighborhood and synagogue school.[1]

Holding that possibility in the back of your mind, recall again that Dismas asked Jesus to remember him in his kingly power. Dismas was willing to wager that this man, whom he may have known all his life, was a king. Hanging there on the cross, dying like that, he did not look like a king to most people. Yet, Dismas knew he was a king and anticipated his exercise of kingly power. So, imagine these two longtime friends arguing down through the years about how best to restore Israel. Perhaps the argument began back in synagogue school and continued throughout their lives whenever their paths crossed. Jesus counseled the way of love and peace. Dismas urged violence and warfare. Here they were now— both revolutionaries of a sort, traveling different paths, urging different tactics, but coming at last to a common death. At that moment Dismas realized that Jesus was right! With a clarity born of extremity, Dismas realized that Jesus was right! Pain pulled off all pretense. Suffering stripped away all superficiality. Agony tore away all appearances. Dismas saw what he himself was—a defeated, sadly mistaken man. Dismas saw what Jesus was—a king! Thus Dismas confronted the commanding, authoritative Jesus and decided he was right. The man on the third cross decided Jesus was wrong. Barabbas struggled to decide—and so must we.

[1] Leslie D. Weatherhead, *Personalities of the Passion* (Nashville: Abingdon Press, 1943), pp. 142-143.

85

MAKING HIM LORD

Dismas did more than decide Jesus was right. He trusted himself to his kingship. It is true that this decision came exceedingly late in the life of Dismas. Having made up his mind about the rightness of Jesus, there was very little of his life left to entrust to him or to bring under his reign. Yet, what was left he did commit. Perhaps it is easier to make Jesus lord of life when little remains than when an indefinite life span stretches out before you. Ours is the harder task. Like Dismas we must decide that Jesus is right and then entrust to him all that remains of our lives. First we make up our minds that he *is* Lord. Then we make up our lives with him *as* Lord.

Let's appear to digress for a moment. Often we say that Jesus saves our souls. It is proper to say that on the cross Jesus saved the soul of Dismas, promising him a place in paradise. However, I think we sometimes play word games with ourselves, talking as we do about the "soul." It is as if we were saying that there is a separate and distinct piece of equipment buried down in each of us called a soul. Jesus takes care of that equipment. He ensures its salvation through a wonderfully mysterious transaction. Yet, it is truer to the Bible to say I *am* a soul than to say I *have* a soul. Rather than simply ensure the eternal safety of an invisible piece of me called a soul, Jesus wants to redeem all of me and take over all of my life. He wants to save not just a piece of me called soul, but all of me, in all of my life and all of my relationships. He wants to rule not just a little fenced-in year of soul-concerns but all of my existence. That may be a simple matter for a man like Dismas who is nailed to a tree and whose life is slipping away from him—not simple in terms of commitment, but simple in terms of effort. For us, there is the not very simple job of bringing every area of life under the lordship of Jesus Christ.

In New York City, a church was preparing to place a new cornerstone. The pastor delved back into history and discovered the first annual report published in 1883. It contained the information that the church had eighty-eight members and that the average attendance at prayer meeting was forty-five and two-thirds percent.[2] One wonders about a man who was two-thirds present at prayer meeting. Yet, speaking of fractions, how much of

[2] Ralph W. Sockman, *The Unemployed Carpenter* (New York: Harper & Row, Publishers, 1933), p. 11.

each of us is actually under the lordship of Jesus Christ? We may have made up our minds that he is right, but have we made up our lives with him as Lord? Over how much of our lives is he in fact Lord? Maybe forty-five and two-thirds percent?

We are told when the Emperor Constantine decided that he was going to be a Christian and his whole empire as well, he arranged for mass baptisms of his army. Entire platoons were baptized at a time. However, the ingenious soldiers devised ways of withholding their swords. And what have we withheld? What part of our lives is still unbaptized? What portion is still not under the lordship of Jesus Christ? Dismas had little to withhold, but we have much more. Maybe it's the billfold or purse—we haven't brought the earning and spending of money under his lordship yet. Perhaps it's our attitude about other races and peoples—we haven't yet brought our prejudices under his lordship. Maybe it's our disposition—we are supercritical or hypersensitive and haven't yet baptized the disposition. We are deceiving ourselves if we believe Jesus is content to save some small portion of us or to exercise rule over a piece of us called "soul." He wants the whole thing. He wants to rule our whole lives.

That is not so simple. We may decide he is right, making up our minds that he *is* Lord and King. But it is a difficult, lifelong task to make up our lives with him *as* Lord and King. Dismas had a short time left to work on that. Ours is the larger, longer task of bringing every area, every phase of our lives under his lordship. Gandhi once told a missionary that his throne was still vacant. While Dismas was hanging there on the cross, he put Jesus on his throne. Barabbas said essentially what Gandhi did. His decision was not yet made; his Lord not yet chosen. Where does the matter rest with *us?* It is not enough that we decide that Jesus is right. We must move on to crown him as Lord. If, in fact, we are at some point along that way, it may encourage us to remember as Barabbas surely could never forget—*someone has died for us.*

87

"Son, behold your mother. . . ."

10. A Man Tied Down

Scripture: John 19:25-27

INTRODUCTION

Few followers risked being at the crucifixion. Most of the disciples were conspicuous by their absence. But John was there. We know he was there because a portion of the third word from the cross was spoken directly to him. We know him as John the beloved disciple. However, few people before that day of the cross would have called him that. Most people would have called him John the angry disciple, or the impetuous disciple, or the impulsive disciple. There is little in the New Testament record prior to the crucifixion that would justify picturing John as either lovely or lovable.

He was a young man, possibly several years younger than Jesus. With his brother James, he was a fisherman working in his father's thriving, prosperous business. The two of them probably were the most wealthy of the disciples. Yet it was not their wealth that singled them out among the twelve. It was their disposition. Jesus gave them a nickname. He called them "sons of thunder," and that they were. John had a violent temper. Angered once at an inhospitable village, he urged Jesus to call down fire from above to destroy it. He had great ambitions. Anxious to get ahead he sought a promise from Jesus that he would have a chief place in the coming kingdom. He showed a measure of intolerance. One time

89

when he saw another man doing good, a man not numbered among the disciple band, he urged Jesus to stop him.

So, to be truthful, the gospel portrait of John is not a totally attractive one. Yet, there is good reason to believe that this was in fact the same John who later wrote so much about love—the same John who became known as the apostle of love. Something happened to him, something dramatic and traumatic. The cross is what happened to him.

John was there that day—big, strong, ambitious, aggressive. He was there, I think, waiting for some final word. He was expecting Jesus to give some last-minute instructions that would make all the difference in the world. So, this John, one-time son of thunder, was there waiting and listening.

INTERVIEW

PREACHER: John, wasn't it dangerous for you to be out there?

JOHN: Of course it was, but that didn't keep me away.

PREACHER: Do I detect a bit of bitterness in that?

JOHN: More than a bit! Oh, I've long since gotten over it. But I was mad that day.

PREACHER: I suspect any friend of Jesus would have been mad at his enemies.

JOHN: Sure—but I think I was madder at his friends than I was at his enemies.

PREACHER: You can't mean that, really!

JOHN: Yes, I mean it! Where were they? You tell me—where were they? I saw only five of us there—four women and me. As far as I know, I was the only disciple there.

PREACHER: Yes, but you've already admitted it was fairly dangerous for any of you to be there. Weren't you taking chances?

JOHN: Of course I was taking chances, but it was worth it.

PREACHER: Worth it, how?

JOHN: Well, Jesus kept looking over the crowd as if he were hunting for somebody. Frankly, I think he was looking for the rest of the disciples—but he didn't find them. They weren't there. At least I was there!

PREACHER: Do you think Jesus knew you were there?

JOHN: Of course he knew I was there. He spoke to me.

PREACHER: You mean he actually singled you out of that crowd and said something specifically to you?

JOHN: That's what I mean.

PREACHER: It must have been a fairly important message.

JOHN: That's the peculiar thing about it all. It didn't seem important at first. To be honest with you, I was rather disappointed.

PREACHER: Disappointed? How?

JOHN: There I was, risking my neck, hoping that Jesus might say something important, and then, when he did speak to me, it didn't seem important at all.

PREACHER: What was it he said?

JOHN: He asked me to take care of his mother. That certainly wasn't what I expected!

PREACHER: What did you expect?

JOHN: I thought he'd tell me what to do. I was ready to go! I was waiting for him to say the word. I would have gotten the disciples together and we would have done something.

PREACHER: But he didn't say the word?

JOHN: No—there I was, ready to turn the world upside down, and he told me to stay home and take care of his mother.

PREACHER: I can see why you were disappointed.

JOHN: Oh, I didn't stay disappointed. Remember, I said that what he said didn't seem important at the time.

PREACHER: Then you changed your mind later?

JOHN: Yes, I guess Jesus knew me pretty well. He knew I'd be mad, that I'd be all set to do something dramatic or violent. So he gave me somebody to take care of instead.

PREACHER: And you did?

JOHN: Yes, I took care of Mary, and I learned my lesson.

PREACHER: What lesson was that?

JOHN: That there may be something more important than turning the world upside down—something like loving one person.

INTERPRETATION

John said he learned his lesson. Surely it wasn't an easy lesson to learn. He must have felt terribly frustrated that day. He wanted so much to hear marching orders and heard instead, "Son, behold your mother." What an unfortunate thing to happen! What a foolish waste of manpower! Saddling a warrior with the care of a widow! But John says he learned his lesson.

91

PARTICULARITY

Jesus gave John a lesson in particularity. If we have understood him correctly, this volatile disciple was ready to lead a movement. He was prepared to march out under the banner of some cause. Jesus brought him down to earth fast! He spoke very few words, but he said in effect: "John, I know you and I know how you feel. You want to do something—and do something big right now. But don't get so wrapped up in big things—big causes and movements—that you forget about the particulars or lose sight of individuals. Take care of that woman standing next to you." That's a lesson in particularity.

On one occasion a lawyer was talking to Jesus. Together they agreed on a summary of the law as love of God and love of neighbor. Then the lawyer asked, "And who is my neighbor?" It appeared that the lawyer was more interested in debate than he was in the neighbor. He wanted to discuss with Jesus the ins and outs of the concept of neighborliness. However, Jesus became very specific and particular and told the story of the man who went down from Jerusalem to Jericho and fell among robbers (Luke 10: 25-37). That, too, was a lesson in particularity. The lawyer may have been ready to discuss for hours on end the cause or plight of the neighbor, but Jesus said, "Be a neighbor to a person in need."

During the years of the Civil War here in the United States, Senator Charles Sumner had great plans for the abolition of slavery. He was completely absorbed in those plans. One time he was asked by Julia Ward Howe to meet some friends. He declined saying, "Really, Julia, I have lost all interest in individuals." She answered, "Why, Charles! God hasn't got as far as that yet." [1] She was trying to give him a lesson in particularity. The abolition of slavery was a great and worthy cause, but the senator should have been interested in individuals and slaves one by one in particular.

Jesus said, "John, in all your ambitious, aggressive desire to do something big and great, don't forget that sad mother over there. Take care of her in particular." It is possible for a person to espouse a great cause and neglect the particulars. A person, for example, may have a great passion for racial justice. He may say all the right things, go to all the right meetings, and enlist in all the right

---

[1] Harry Emerson Fosdick, *Living Under Tension* (New York: Harper & Row, Publishers, 1941), p. 199.

movements. Yet he may fail ever to befriend a particular individual of another race. Such a person needs a lesson in particularity. A woman may be greatly concerned about peace. She may wish an end to all the hellish business of making war and strongly support all peacemaking efforts. Yet she may fail ever to make peace with her next-door neighbor. Such a person needs a lesson in particularity. A man may be very alarmed over the specter of poverty in the land. He may write his congressman, agitate for legislation, and march for the poor. Yet he may fail ever to provide a job for one man in his own organization or ever to adopt one needy family. Such a person needs a lesson in particularity. John was given such a lesson. His was the cause of Christ. His was the kingdom of love. But there was a particular mother who needed loving. Sooner or later all grandiose talk about love and brotherhood and the kingdom and peace had better get down to particulars. It did for John. It must for us.

AUTHENTICITY

Jesus gave John a lesson in particularity and a lesson in authenticity. This was not so much a different lesson as a second installment of the same lesson. Jesus spoke very few words to John, but he said in effect, "John, all of your concerns about the big things of the kingdom will not be authentic unless things are right at home. Take this grieving woman home with you. Love and care for her." Here was Jesus on the cross with the love of the world in his heart. Yet if he had failed to act lovingly toward this mother of his, would that larger love have seemed as authentic?

Bishop Gerald Kennedy tells of a woman who needed this lesson in authenticity. He writes that she

had more real concern for the big causes than any individual I have ever known. She would spend any time necessary to organize a group or to serve on a committee, if it had a world-wide program. She would take the time to write letters to her Congressman expressing her opinion about pending legislation. But her home was always a mess, and the children never looked quite clean or very well tended. The meals were haphazard affairs, which provided nourishment but no aesthetic pleasure. Her husband always impressed me as a man who suffered from low spirits. Sometimes it seemed to me that in her desire to serve something far away she was overlooking her most important calling right in her own home.[2]

---

[2] Gerald Kennedy, *Who Speaks for God?* (Nashville: Abingdon Press, 1954), pp. 30-31.

The Bishop is saying that the lady lacked authenticity—her home front betrayed her public image. She needed the same lesson in authenticity that Jesus administered to John. My sister, Lois, knew some others who needed it, too. In her 'teenage years, she did considerable baby-sitting. One couple used her services frequently. She dreaded the nights at that home—the children of the family were terrors, 100 percent rascals. She did battle with the children while the mother and father went out to lecture on child rearing and family life. The parents needed a lesson in authenticity.

Someone has suggested that we utilize our imaginations and picture John arriving in heaven. He is met there by Jesus. Immediately he begins telling Jesus that he has been busy working in His kingdom. Jesus asks, "How's Mother?" John goes on as if not hearing, telling all he accomplished in kingdom work. Again Jesus asks, "But how is my mother?" Then John confesses that he has been too busy really to think about Mary, but insists that he has gotten much done. Would Jesus then say, "Well done, John, good and faithful servant"? No, we don't think so. John would have missed the point of the word Jesus spoke to him from the cross. It was a lesson in authenticity. Sooner or later all our talk about love and brotherhood and the kingdom and peace and all of that had better be reflected in the way we live or act at home and in our most intimate relationships. It was for John. It must be for us.

So Jesus with an amazing economy of words taught this ambitious, aggressive son of thunder some important lessons: a lesson in particularity and a lesson in authenticity. John learned those lessons so well that succeeding generations have called him the apostle of love. There is a legend about John. Tradition says he lived to an extreme old age. He was carried to church. Feeble as he was, he said little. When he did speak, it always was the same thing, "Little children, love one another." At length the others wearied of hearing the same words again and again. They asked, "Master, why [do you] always say this?" He replied, "It is the Lord's command, and, if this alone be done, it is enough!"[3] Well, that's what Jesus was teaching John that day. Love one another, and begin by loving that particular grieving mother right there next to you. Surely that's what he would have all of us learn. "Love one another, and begin by loving that one right there next to you, near you in the pew, or near you at home."

[3] William Barclay, *The Master's Men* (Nashville: Abingdon Press, 1959), p. 38.

94

"My God, my God, why . . . ?"

11. A Follower Proved Human

Scripture: Matthew 26:30-35; Mark 15:33-34

INTRODUCTION

The twelve disciples were normal human beings. We do them an injustice if we think of them as otherwise. They had no special spiritual organs to make them more susceptible to the faith. They were not endowed with any unusual equipment of the soul to predispose them to conversion. They lived in intimate contact with Jesus for many months and yet did not find it easy to follow his way or even to understand it. One was a skeptic by nature, and after three years with Jesus he still needed physical proof or he would not believe. Others were ambitious and, in spite of Christ's counsel to the contrary, openly sought power and prestige. One was a mistaken revolutionary, and long exposure to the gentle Jesus left him essentially unchanged. Others were unmoved by Christ's sense of urgency and remained lukewarm and dispassionate. They were ordinary men of their day, struggling to follow a new master.

Peter is a symbol of the twelve. He is a symbol of their humanness, of the problems they faced, of the depths to which they sank, and of the heights which they attained. At no time is his humanness more apparent than in the last week of his Master's life. Jesus had predicted that all the disciples would fall away and that Peter would deny him. That brought strong protests from

95

Peter—but deny him he did. He must have been terribly distressed by his denials, tortured by his disloyalty.

Let it be said that the failures of Peter were the failures of the brave. He was recognized in the high priest's courtyard and accosted by one of the maids, but he was there. Evidently no one else had had the courage to draw that near. The others were safely hidden away, afraid to be anywhere near the scene of the trial. But not Peter—he was there, throwing caution to the winds, knowing that at any moment he might be recognized and seized. One cannot honor Peter for his denials, but one must honor him for the courage that brought him to that dangerous place.

Somehow I feel that same bravery brought Peter to the crucifixion. True, the New Testament provides no support for such a suggestion. Yet, if Peter could not stay away from the high priest's house, how could he have remained away from Golgotha? Wouldn't Peter have been especially anxious to be there in view of his denials? I picture him there, probably disguised, eager for some reassurance.

INTERVIEW

PREACHER: Peter, those were hellish days for you.

PETER: Yes, they were—and they still seem like a nightmare to me.

PREACHER: I guess you sometimes wonder how it all happened.

PETER: Of course, especially how some of it happened to me.

PREACHER: I suppose you're referring to your troubles there in the high priest's courtyard.

PETER: Troubles? Why so polite? They were denials! I may have had the best intentions but I ended up denying him!

PREACHER: Well, I admire your honesty, but what did you intend?

PETER: Nothing very complicated! I thought one of the disciples should be there to see what was going on. I hoped to slip in unnoticed and sort of spy on things.

PREACHER: And then you got caught?

PETER: Yes, I did—and then I got frightened and lost my head and said some things I've never been able to live down.

PREACHER: I'm sorry about that, but do you think Jesus knew what was going on with you that night?

PETER: I know he did. He even told me earlier he thought I'd find it difficult to stick by him. Yet I never thought I'd forsake him that way.

96

PREACHER: Forsake? Is that what you'd call it?

PETER: That fairly well describes it. I denied that I knew him and forsook him and ran away.

PREACHER: You must have felt devastated!

PETER: I was more worried about how Jesus felt.

PREACHER: How do you mean?

PETER: I was worried that Jesus would think everyone had deserted him—and I think he did feel that way.

PREACHER: What makes you think that?

PETER: Something he said on the cross.

PREACHER: People heard him say a number of things. Did you have something particular in mind?

PETER: Yes, I did.

PREACHER: Could you tell me about it?

PETER: You have to remember how I was feeling. I had this terrible feeling of guilt. I wondered if Jesus would ever forgive me. And then he said, "My God, my God, why have you forsaken me?"

PREACHER: That must have startled you!

PETER: I'll say it did. It wouldn't have surprised me if he'd said, "Peter, why did you forsake me?" But God? I wasn't expecting that!

PREACHER: What did you make of that?

PETER: I knew then just how bad he really felt. He had reason to feel forsaken by me and the others—but I guess I never thought he'd feel forsaken by God.

INTERPRETATION

Peter helps us feel the stark reality of that forsakenness. Those words startled Peter and they have staggered the Christian community. They stand at the center of the seven words from the cross and have been called the crucifixion within the crucifixion, the tragedy within the tragedy. We expect Christ to be forgiving of his enemies, to offer paradise to a dying thief, and to be thoughtful of his grieving mother. But we, as well as Peter, do not expect this word of godforsakenness. George Buttrick says that to ask too many questions or to probe too deeply is "like geologizing on holy ground."[1] Yet we intend to do some of that and hope that Peter did

[1] George A. Buttrick, "Exposition of Matthew," *The Interpreter's Bible*, vol. 7 (Nashville: Abingdon Press, 1951), p. 607.

97

too. Here is not only the awful reality of godforsakenness, but also the revelation of how Jesus handled those feelings. We will try to do some reverent geologizing on that holy ground.

FACING THE FEELINGS

Note this at the outset: Jesus faced his feelings! Throughout the centuries, some of his followers have had difficulty facing the fact he actually had those feelings. The words themselves are crammed full of feeling. Various attempts have been made to soften their impact or explain them away. Their unexpectedness commends their authenticity to us. A German scholar once made a list of biblical passages that could not have been invented. This was among them. No one ever would have invented words like these. No writer would have dared to concoct these words and put them on the lips of Jesus. The very fact that this fourth word is so difficult and unexpected testifies to its genuineness. We may be reluctant to face his feelings of forsakenness, but he was not. That's what this word is all about. Jesus, I believe, uttered this word precisely because it expressed his genuine feelings at the time. I think we must accept the harsh reality of his feelings of godforsakenness. I prefer not to be overly theological about it. John Calvin suggested that Christ felt forsaken because he was forsaken. On the cross Jesus voluntarily took upon himself the sins of the whole world. God, of course, forsakes sin and thus he necessarily forsook Christ. Calvin argued, therefore, that Christ felt forsaken because he was forsaken. I prefer not to be that theological about it. Here was a man in a horrible hell of pain. Of course he felt alone. Pain does that to anyone. There was nothing very complex or theological about it. Jesus was a man in the extremity of agony. He felt alone. He felt forsaken by one and all.

It is common knowledge that these words, "My God, my God, why have you forsaken me?" are the words with which Psalm 22 begins. We can assume Jesus was quoting this ancient Hebrew poetry. Yet I think he quoted it precisely because it expressed how he felt. He felt forsaken and he used poetry to verbalize it. Let's not try to explain that away. Here Christ draws near to us. Here Christ is one with us. No being, no person sharing our human lot could be falsely accused, maltreated, and nailed to a tree without feeling forsaken. This Jesus, with his feelings of forsakenness, is one of us,

98

one with us. This was no phony operation, no make-believe. This was real suffering and real forsakenness.

This word has been called a cry of dereliction. That is strong language. Derelict means abandoned. A derelict ship is a ship completely deserted, drifting about without course or direction. Jesus felt deserted, abandoned, forsaken—and out of those feelings honestly faced came this cry of dereliction. In that, Jesus joined us in our humanity. Of course we feel forsaken from time to time. Things happen to us. Misfortune visits us or our loved ones. Tragedy strikes; disaster befalls us. It is best that we, like Jesus, face those feelings of godforsakenness. Jesus cried out *to* God, and cries *with* us: "My God, my God, why have you forsaken me?" Jesus faced his feelings of forsakenness. But more, and I think this is the secret, he faced God with those feelings.

FACING GOD WITH THE FEELINGS

Jesus faced his feelings of forsakenness, but he did more than that. He did something with those feelings. He did not allow them to destroy his faith or to capsize his spirit. He faced God with those feelings. That makes all the difference in the world for him and for us. Remember that this fourth word was addressed to God: "My God, my God. . . ." It was not addressed to the people below, asking them to witness the awfulness of his distress and forsakenness. It was not thrown out into the emptiness of space. It was addressed to God.[2] Jesus was talking to someone. He was talking to God about his feelings of forsakenness. That's the secret. Jesus felt forsaken— forsaken by men, yea, even forsaken by God. However, he did not turn away from God, but toward God. He did not talk to men about his forsakenness, saying, "Look what it gets you. I serve God all my life and here I am forsaken." He talked to God and faced God with his feelings. He still clung to his God in his forsakenness. He still had his God in his forsakenness.[3] It was as if he were saying, "My God, I feel forsaken right now. Yet I know I am not forsaken, for you are still my God." A man who in his forsakenness turns toward God and prayerfully implores him is not forsaken. He may feel forsaken, but deep down he knows he is not.

[2] Robert F. Jones, *Seven Words to the Cross* (Richmond: John Knox Press, 1961), p. 60.

[3] Helmut Thielicke has an interesting discussion of this in *Christ and the Meaning of Life* (New York: Harper & Row, Publishers, 1962), pp. 45-46.

99

J. B. Phillips made a discovery about the verb in this fourth word.[4] As we know, our New Testament passed through several languages in the process of coming to us in English. From Hebrew, it was translated into Greek, and from Greek into English. Phillips says that some Hebrew authorities think that the tense of the verb has been tampered with in this transmission process. We have it this way: "My God, my God, why have you forsaken me?" These scholars suggest that it ought to be: "My God, my God, why did you forsake me?" That may seem like an insignificant change. However, in the former, Jesus speaks out of a present state of forsakenness. In the latter, he speaks as if the forsakenness were past. I like that change in verbs. It doesn't alter my understanding of the word; it supports it. According to the account, this word was spoken after three hours of silence. I can imagine what was going on in the mind of Jesus during those three long hours. His brief life must have paraded before him. "Why? Why did it come out like this?" Of course, he felt forsaken. Yet at the end of those three hours, he had won a victory, a victory over his feelings of forsakenness. I can imagine Jesus searching for some way of sharing with the people down there at the foot of the cross. He searched for a means of sharing with them what had happened to him in those three hours, sharing his awful feelings of forsakenness but sharing also his victory over them. As he searched, there came to his mind one of the most familiar psalms of his people. It was a psalm that everyone knew, a psalm frequently used in liturgy. He knew the people would understand if he repeated that. It was a psalm that began with feelings of forsakenness and misery but ended with faith and trust. So he began a message to those people, a message that his waning strength prevented finishing. "I feel forsaken, and you may think me forsaken, but I am not. I still have my God."

Some say that's a fanciful interpretation. Men in dying agony, they argue, are not given to reciting poetry. I disagree. I have been a pastor long enough and have witnessed sufficient suffering and dying to know that men do turn to poetry or Scripture in their darkest hours. I have watched scores of people face pain and death softly repeating, "The Lord is my shepherd. . . ." Here on the cross Jesus was doing what men for ages before him and for centuries

---

[4] J. B. Phillips, *Good News* (New York: The Macmillan Company, 1963), p. 183.

since him have done—turning to great words of the past to express feelings of the present. He felt forsaken, genuinely forsaken. There was nothing phony about those feelings. Yet he turned toward God, rather than away from him, with those feelings. And that I think was the secret of his winning through.

You may feel forsaken right now. You may feel that the bottom of life has dropped out. Don't turn away from God with those feelings; turn toward him. You may feel abandoned and rejected. You may feel that no one loves you or cares for you, not even God. Don't turn away from God with those feelings; turn toward him. You may be full of doubt. You may be asking, "Is there a God? Can I believe? Is life worth living?" Don't turn away from God with those feelings; turn toward him. Obviously it is not wrong to have those feelings. Jesus himself had them. The secret is to face those feelings and then face God with those feelings.

We talk about touching wood or knocking on wood. We call that a superstition. The people who do it believe that it brings them good luck or prevents bad luck. Recently I learned about the source of that practice. In ancient times, many of the most devout had what they thought were splinters from the cross of Jesus. They carried these splinters with them at all times or wore them on chains about their necks. To touch the wood was to remind them of the courage of Jesus and to bring new courage to them. Touching that wood was not good luck for Jesus. But it is our glorious good fortune to stand beneath that wood today and know that though at times we may feel forsaken, we are in fact never forsaken. A man who talks to God about his forsakenness still has his God.

"I thirst."

12. A Woman Set Wondering

Scripture: Matthew 27:33-36; John 19:28-29

INTRODUCTION

A great multitude of people gathered for the crucifixion that day. One writer suggests that we put the event on canvas, using colors to represent emotions. If we do so, it becomes quite a scene. There were those "red with anger, purple with rage, green with envy, yellow with cowardice, blue with loyalty, white with purity, black with shame, and gray with indecision."[1] They were all there. We may wonder why. After all, it was not a very pleasant thing to watch. Crucifixion was designed not simply to put a man to death but to disgrace utterly and desecrate his life. It began with the scourging. The victim was bound to a column or pole. His naked back was lashed with a whip or knotted leather thongs. The soldiers had their own techniques for increasing the agony. Occasionally a victim failed to survive the scourging and thus was spared the cross. Once at the site of the crucifixion, there was the horror of nails driven through flesh and the awful jarring as the cross was lifted and dropped into place. Unless Jesus was treated with special dignity, and we have no reason to assume that he was, he was completely naked. His cross probably held him but a few

[1] Paul L. Moore, *Seven Words of Men Around the Cross* (Nashville: Abingdon Press, 1963), p. 11.

103

inches from the ground to heighten the disgrace of it all. No, it was not a very pleasant sight to watch.

The book of Hebrews says of Jesus that he "endured the cross, despising the shame" (Hebrews 12:2). *The New English Bible* says he "endured the cross, making light of its disgrace." There was pain to be endured, and more disgrace than one could be expected to "make light of." The executioners not only put him to death, they sought to disgrace his life. Who would want to watch all that? Not I! If I had been a close friend of a victim, I might have wanted to be present. Otherwise, I would not have been there unless I was required to be. Apparently some were so required. This was no place for women, but women were there. Some by choice: Mary and a few close friends. Others were there because they had a job to do. I'm going to talk with one of those women.

INTERVIEW

PREACHER: I'm sorry. I don't know your name.

WOMAN: That's all right. I prefer it that way.

PREACHER: You mean you would just as soon I didn't know your name? You'd rather be anonymous?

WOMAN: That's right.

PREACHER: Why? Any particular reason?

WOMAN: Oh, I don't know. I felt mixed up about what went on out there. I'm not sure I want to be associated with it.

PREACHER: Did you have a special reason for being there?

WOMAN: Yes. I was supposed to be there.

PREACHER: You mean you weren't there just out of curiosity?

WOMAN: No, no, I wouldn't have been there unless I'd had to be.

PREACHER: I don't understand. Why did you have to be there?

WOMAN: Well—a group of us women from the temple attended all crucifixions—not because we wanted to watch but because we wanted to help.

PREACHER: How could you help with a crucifixion?

WOMAN: We didn't help with crucifixions! We helped the victims!

PREACHER: How? What could you do for them?

WOMAN: It was our job to make a special drink for them. It was a mixture of wine and some other things, myrrh for example. It was a rather strong drink really. The idea was to deaden the pain. The victim drank it and that way he could stand the pain a little better.

104

PREACHER: That seems like a kind thing to do. I suspect the victims were glad to have that drink.

WOMAN: Yes, generally they were, but not this Jesus.

PREACHER: What do you mean?

WOMAN: Jesus wouldn't drink it. We offered it to him but he wouldn't drink it. That's the only time I can ever remember that somebody wouldn't drink it.

PREACHER: What did you make of that?

WOMAN: It was rather odd. At first we thought it was going to be terrible. We thought he wouldn't be able to take it. Some victims even with the drink did a lot of screaming and yelling. So we expected the worst.

PREACHER: What did happen?

WOMAN: Nothing—at least nothing like we expected. I don't think we'd ever seen a man die so calmly, and that started us wondering.

PREACHER: Wondering about what?

WOMAN: We wondered if he was human. I know it sounds odd, and you'll probably think we were just silly women, but we really wondered if he was human.

PREACHER: What else could he have been?

WOMAN: We didn't know. Some folks said he was the Messiah or something like that. It just didn't seem human for a man to be able to take all that. Yet in other ways he seemed human.

PREACHER: How do you mean?

WOMAN: Well, he spoke to his mother there. Like any normal son, he said some kind things to her.

PREACHER: Anything else?

WOMAN: Yes, later on he said he was thirsty. That seemed peculiar to us. He refused our drink as if he didn't hurt like a normal human being. Then later he said he was thirsty.

PREACHER: I guess you women had something to talk about for a while.

WOMAN: Yes—but I don't know whether we ever got any place with all our talking. I told you I was kind of mixed up about it. I just don't know—I can't quite figure out what was going on.

INTERPRETATION

The woman has our sympathies. She complained of not being able to figure out what was happening. Generations of men have

105

had difficulty fully understanding it. In one of McGuffey's Readers there is a story about a certain gentleman who attended church one Sunday. That morning the preacher's subject was the crucifixion. It was a most impressive and learned sermon. In it the minister contrasted the death of Jesus with the death of Socrates. Over and over again, the preacher rang the changes on this word: "Socrates died like a philosopher; Jesus died like a God." Says one commentator, "The preacher was wrong!" He died like a man, not like a God.[2] Yet there were people present and listening who saw in him almost superhuman forbearance. How could a normal human being take all that without striking back? And they saw in him almost superhuman concern too. How could an ordinary human be so concerned about others in the extremity of his own agony? Yet in the midst of all of that superhuman forbearance and concern was this very human, very ordinary plea, "I thirst!" With that simple word, Jesus removed all doubt about his oneness with us and his presence with us, too.

HIS ONENESS WITH US

Jesus said, "I thirst," and with that word removed all doubt about his oneness with us! With this word he made clear that he shares our humanity, shares it to the fullest extent. He shares our human extremity; shares our humanness in knowing pain, suffering, and agony; shares the worst that can come to man. This word is a word of pain. This is not simply the expression of the impulse that drives us to the fountain or faucet frequently throughout the day, there to gulp a few swallows of cold, refreshing water. This word is the admission of terrible pain. Crucifixion, as we indicated before, was not chosen as a merciful way to execute criminals. It was chosen because it could inflict so much pain over so long a time. Part of the punishment was the exposure of the body to the blistering sunlight hour after hour. Of course, the lips were parched, the throat dry. Those who have had major surgery, or who have watched beside the bed of another who has, know something about thirst and pain. The first thing the patient wants after coming out of the anesthesia is a drink of water. A moistened cloth is placed to the lips, then some cracked ice, and finally a sip of water. Jesus said, "I thirst." He was saying, "I hurt. I

[2]Clovis G. Chappell, *The Seven Words* (Nashville: Abingdon Press, 1952), p. 40.

106

know pain. I know what it is to suffer. I share man's extremity." After such a word, could there be any doubt of his oneness with us in our humanity?

In the early centuries, there was a peculiar heresy which held that Jesus was not authentically human and had no human body. This heresy said Jesus was pure spirit in a phantom body. So they suggested, for example, that when he walked about the earth, his feet left no footprints. But phantom bodies don't get thirsty. Jesus removed all doubt that he was one with man. We customarily say two things about life are certain: death and taxes. We could add a third: pain. It, too, is one of the universals. It is a rare human life that has not plumbed the depths of some kind of pain. Pain is of the very nature of humanity. And Jesus says: "I know it. I, too, have plumbed its depths. I, too, have thirsted. I, too, have walked in a dry and thirsty land where no water is."

It is to be remembered that pain is not an unrelieved curse. It may be the worst that can happen to man, but it makes possible the best that can happen to him, too. The same sensitivity that makes pain possible, also makes pleasure possible. It is man's sensitivity, or his capacity for sensitivity, which marks him as the noblest of nature's creatures. It is because man is sensitive and therefore subject to pain and suffering that it is possible for him to know and share goodness, beauty, truth, and love. Pain and pleasure issue from the same sensitivity. "Pain is the price of sensitivity," wrote an English pastor. "It is the higher forms of life that feel it most . . . but those same forms of higher life have compensations. It is from their nervous systems, wonderfully co-ordinated, incredibly alert, that they are aware of the varied delights of sensory perception."[3] He is arguing that the price of sensitivity to beauty, pleasure, and such is the possibility of pain.

Harry Emerson Fosdick points out that long ago in the process of creation there were small creatures, something like oysters. Their skeletons were on the outside and their nerves were on the inside, protected so they wouldn't have to suffer. However, the progress of nature left them behind. Then a new experiment was tried: man, a creature with his bones on the inside and his nerves on the outside where he could be sensitive and know pain. It is this

[3] Leslie Badham, *Love Speaks from the Cross* (Nashville: Abingdon Press, 1955), p. 45.

107

sensitive, pain-bearing creature that is nature's and God's best.[4] Best because it can suffer. Best because it can know pain. Best because from a cross it can cry, "I thirst."

In Aldous Huxley's Brave New World we meet a character called Savage. He is a hero of sorts. In the brave new world, the inhabitants are given a drug called soma. Soma makes the people oblivious to, or insensitive to, unpleasantness in all forms. However, Savage refuses to take the drug. Instead, he claims "the right to be tortured by unspeakable pains of every kind."[5] He was claiming the right to suffer because he knew that was in actuality the right to be a sensitive human being. Perhaps nothing says this better than the familiar yet ancient legend about the lady who approached the River Styx. She, as every mortal eventually was, was to be ferried across the river to the region of departed spirits. The kindly ferryman suggested to her that it was her privilege to drink of the waters of Lethe and thus forget the life she was leaving behind. She said, "I will forget how I have suffered." "Yes," said the ferryman, "and how you have rejoiced." She said, "I will forget my failures." "Yes, and your victories too," "I will forget how I have been hated." "Yes," said the ferryman, "and how you have been loved too." She decided not to drink. She would not give up the memory of love, rejoicing, and victory in order to be free of the memory of hate, suffering, and failure.[6] The same sensitivity which makes us susceptible to pain makes us responsive to good and pleasure. We can't have one without the other. Jesus said, "I thirst," and removed all doubt about his oneness with us in all of this. He made clear that he shares our common human lot of sensitivity.

HIS PRESENCE WITH US

That is not all he did with that word. He also removed all doubt about his presence with us. It is not simply that Jesus shares our common human lot of suffering and pain. He not only shares it, he does something to it. He sheds light on it and consecrates it. Pain and suffering can never be the same again, never—because there

[4] Harry Emerson Fosdick, Successful Christian Living (Garden City: Garden City Books, 1953), p. 201.

[5] Aldous Huxley, Brave New World (New York: Bantam Books, Inc., 1960), p. 163. Used with permission of Harper & Row, Publishers, Inc.

[6] Ralph W. Sockman, The Higher Happiness (Nashville: Abingdon Press, 1950), p. 43.

was this cross. The cross has done something to pain. Christ has in some mysterious way consecrated it. He has consecrated it and revealed some of the secret of bearing it. Jesus did not allow the pain to rob him of his self-control. The pain, no matter how intense, did not twist and warp his mind. Even in pain he thought first of others: the men who had nailed him there, the criminal on the next cross, his mother. Pain was not a thief stealing away his values and deforming his very self. A part of the secret of his mastery of pain was his ability to hold on to himself. That could be a good word of counsel for us, too. Further, he did not simply grit his teeth and bear the suffering and pain with a kind of stoical pride. He didn't scream out or groan incessantly as some are given to doing. Yet he had no hesitation in speaking of it. He said, "I suffer. I hurt. I thirst." He didn't try to disguise his discomfort or make believe that he wasn't in agony. There was nothing of the idea that the best way to handle pain is to keep it welled up within yourself as a secret you dare not let out lest you reveal a weakness. No, he took pain seriously as something that needed to be frankly accepted and openly acknowledged. It was not something to be nurtured in unnatural isolation, but something to be mastered through acceptance and acknowledgment. That might be a word of counsel for us too. Still further, and this is most important, he has done something to pain and suffering for you and for me. He has made them into a kind of sacrament, a sacrament of his presence. Whenever we suffer, that suffering can be a sacrament of his presence as we remember his suffering. Whenever we are in pain, that pain can be a sacrament of his presence as he enters our hearts to be our companion in pain.

With this simple word, "I thirst!" Jesus removed all doubt about his oneness with us and his presence with us.

"It is finished."

13. A Soldier Turned Thoughtful

Scripture: John 19:29-30; Mark 15:39

INTRODUCTION

A Roman centurion witnessed the last hours and heard the last words of Jesus. He would have been in charge of the execution squad. We are not certain of his name, but tradition has called him Longinus. A centurion was the commanding officer of one hundred foot soldiers in the Roman army. He was a career man, commonly referred to as the backbone of the troops. Generally, he came up through the ranks and was a man of considerable experience and ability. He was transferred frequently from one spot to another. Consequently, a centurion was cosmopolitan in outlook and generally well informed. His was the highest and best rank to which an ordinary soldier could aspire.

Actually, centurions fare quite well in the New Testament record. There are some three or four specific references to them. Each of these references is in an appreciative spirit. For example, it was to a centurion whose servant he had healed that Jesus said, "Truly, I say to you, not even in Israel have I found such faith" (Matthew 8:10). The centurion was not classed among the vulgar, the base, the unlearned. Rather, he was respected as a fairly decent sort of person, a man with principles. Such was Longinus: every bit a man—a wise, capable, practical young man. He was there doing his duty at a public execution.

111

INTERVIEW

PREACHER: Longinus, I guess you were in charge out there at the crucifixion?

LONGINUS: That's right. I drew the detail that day.

PREACHER: That wasn't your first crucifixion, was it?

LONGINUS: Oh, no! I'd had a hand in a good many.

PREACHER: Did you have any particular feelings about doing that sort of thing?

LONGINUS: Not really. It was part of a day's work for a soldier.

PREACHER: You sound kind of calloused to me.

LONGINUS: Well, you have to be. I don't make the decisions. I'm under orders. They tell me to nail a man to a cross, and I nail him to a cross.

PREACHER: I suppose you get used to it after while.

LONGINUS: Yes, but no two crucifixions were the same.

PREACHER: How do you mean? Didn't you do the same thing every time?

LONGINUS: We did—the soldiers I mean. We had a set procedure we followed. But you never knew what the prisoner was going to do.

PREACHER: I would think that there was something similar about all criminal types.

LONGINUS: You might think so—but I found that no two men died alike. Look at what happened that day. We executed three men, and each one died in his own special way.

PREACHER: You sound like an observant man.

LONGINUS: I don't know about that, but I think you can tell a lot about the way a man has lived by the way he dies.

PREACHER: Now you sound like a philosopher.

LONGINUS: Me? That's a laugh. I just know from experience that some men die one way and others die another way. Some guys crumble and some stand up. Some are brave and some are cowards. When you're dying like that, it shows you up for what you really are.

PREACHER: Would you say then that you were a fairly good judge of character?

LONGINUS: I'd say I knew a real man when I saw one.

PREACHER: You know, Longinus, you've become something of a hero among later Christians?

LONGINUS: How do you mean?

112

PREACHER: Well, our New Testament tells us that you said something fine about Jesus. I guess we remember it because there wasn't much fine said about him that day.

LONGINUS: Oh, that! That's the sort of thing I've been talking about. Jesus died his own special way and it made quite an impression on me.

PREACHER: I guess it must have, saying what you did.

LONGINUS: Why? What do you think I said?

PREACHER: Well, one writer says you said he was a righteous man and another claims you said he was the Son of God. That makes you sound like a theologian.

LONGINUS: Me, a theologian? All I meant was that if this fellow was bad I'd like to see the good ones. I watched him long enough to believe that if he said he was the Son of God, he was the Son of God.

PREACHER: So he was one of the ones that didn't crumble, that stood up fairly well?

LONGINUS: I never saw one any better or braver. If he lived anything like he died, he was a great man.

PREACHER: Our records tell us that Jesus spoke a number of times. Did you hear him?

LONGINUS: I heard every word he said.

PREACHER: Do you remember anything in particular?

LONGINUS: Yes. I'd just given him a taste of sour wine. That seemed to revive him somewhat, and he shouted, "It is finished!"

PREACHER: You think he meant that it was all over for him?

LONGINUS: No. Strangely enough, it sounded more like something a soldier might shout after he'd won a battle. Whatever it was that was finished, he's the one that finished it.

INTERPRETATION

Longinus must have heard that word with unique clarity. He was in a position to hear all the inflections and emotions that were in it. Whatever he heard in it increased his appreciation for this man Jesus. At first hearing, this may seem like a word of resignation or defeat. Jesus probably cried out just one word. When translated into English, it becomes three words. With what must have been a herculean effort, he shouted out his one word: "Finished!" Was it a cry of final agony? Was he saying, "I can take no more; pain and exposure have done their worst"? Was it a cry of relief? "At last, it's about over." Was it a cry of despair? "I'm through, done in, and done for." Or, was it that other kind of cry as Longinus suggested? Was it a cry of victory? Was it a cry on the lips of a man who has won a battle? I believe it was that! I believe it was not a cry of resignation or defeat but a cry of victory and triumph.

"It is finished!" That word "finished" appears in a variety of texts. In the book of Hebrews we are urged to "run with patience the race that is set before us, looking unto Jesus the author and finisher of our faith" (See Hebrews 12:1-2, KJV). The word "finisher" has the same root as the word from the cross. It means the author and perfecter of our faith. In Second Timothy, Paul says, "I have fought a good fight, I have finished my course, I have kept the faith" (2 Timothy 4:7, KJV). Again that word "finished" has the same root. It means "I have completed the course." So Jesus with a shout of triumph cried out: "Finished!"

FINISHED MEANS PERFECTED

We most often try to hear this word from the cross through the ears of people who were there on the scene. Now try to imagine God hearing this word. One interpreter suggests that when God heard this word, he was satisfied for the second time. When God finished creation, he looked out on all he had made and was satisfied: "Behold, it was very good." Then as Jesus breathed his last, God looked down on the finished life of his Son and was satisfied. "Behold, it too was very good."[1] It was finished, perfected. A man had listened to the voice of God, had discovered what life was about, had perfected the business of living. Life itself had been finished, perfected.

It is not uncommon for us to say of a product, "It is all in the finishing." We recognize that two products may be made of the same material. They can be put together in essentially the same way. That which makes one better than the other is the finish put on it. No doubt Joseph took great pains in the carpentry shop to show the boy Jesus how to put the finishing touches on a door frame or an oxen's yoke. Says one, "It is easier to put a finish on a piece of carpentry than to put the mark of excellence on a life."[2]

[1] Leslie Badham, *Love Speaks from the Cross* (Nashville: Abingdon Press, 1955), p. 55.
[2] *Ibid.*, p. 50.

114

Yet that is just what Jesus did. It was finished, perfected. That life had the mark of excellence upon it.

On reflection, it is odd that this life should be called perfect. Think of what it included! It included rejection—his hometown people tried to throw him off a cliff, and his family thought him beside himself. It included temptation, desertion, denial, betrayal, false accusation, and finally criminal execution. What we call the perfect life included all that. And think of what it missed: the love of a wife and family, education and training, job security, social status, longevity. What we call the perfect life missed all that. Suffice it to say, if that life is perfect, we judge ours by other standards. But which standards are right? Which one of us can look back across his life and say, "It is finished, perfected." And if we're given another five, ten, fifteen, twenty, or even fifty years, will we have it finished then? It was said of Jesus that his life could not have been further perfected even had it been further prolonged.[3] Life's perfection doesn't have to do with time, or comforts, or possessions, or the presence or absence of pleasures and sufferings. Life's perfection has to do with rightness with its Creator. Finished means perfected. It meant that to Jesus. What will finished mean to us?

FINISHED MEANS COMPLETED, TOO

We have said that when God heard this word, "It is finished," he may very well have said, "It was good; it was perfect." When Christendom has heard this word, it has said, "It is done; it is completed." Down through the centuries, the Christian household has spoken of "the finished work of Jesus Christ." That's a term rich in tradition and hoary with age. The heart of the gospel has been that Jesus did something there on the cross, finished something, the acceptance of which is necessary to man's reconciliation with God. There are literally hundreds of theories about the finished work of Christ. Book after book has been written about the various doctrines of the atonement. The cross was a mysterious transaction between God, man, and Christ. It was a completed transaction which defies full comprehension.

Let me suggest a simple, uncomplicated understanding. To speak of the finished work of Christ is to say that Christ is God's last word. Not last in the sense of final, but last in the sense of

[3]*Ibid*, p. 52.

115

ultimate. In Christ, God said it all. There is no more to be said, no more to be done. Jesus could say, "It is finished," knowing it was completed, knowing that the ultimate word about God had been spoken. Through him the full truth had been revealed. The way had been finished; the means had been completed. It remains for us to accept what he has finished and walk in the way he has opened.

One writer offers this illustration. Suppose you have a small child in your family. That child comes to you with a gift in his hand. You take the gift gladly and gratefully. Then the child asks, "Now do you love me?" That spoils everything. The poor child is growing up under the illusion that he must win your love or earn your affection.[4] Your desire is that the child grow up in the security of your unfailing love. God is the father; you are the child. He loves you. There is nothing you can do to make him love you more. There is no gift you can bring to increase his love. That part is finished. Christ finished the revelation of God as love—unmerited, undeserved love. Your part is simple acceptance and growing in the security of that love. It is finished, completed. The ultimate word about God has been spoken, and so has the ultimate word about human life.

Imagine a visitor from outer space, suggests one preacher. The visitor in due course of time becomes aware of the problems of earth. He sees the difficulties men have in getting along with each other. He observes violence, war, brutality, the strange specter of poverty and plenty side by side. Finally, he asks, "Don't men know better? Haven't they been taught a better way?" Man replies, "Yes, we know a better way—we have been taught a better way but that was two thousand years ago and men forget." Whereupon the visitor leaves, saying as he goes, "I must leave lest this foolishness be contagious. I will return in a thousand years or so to see if you have made any progress."[5] It is finished, completed. The ultimate word about life has been spoken. We need not search for another way or a new way. We need only to walk in it. Finished means perfected. The perfect finish has been put on a life. Finished means completed. The ultimate word about God and life has been spoken.

[4] Noah M. Inbody, "The Seven Last Words," Part 6, *The Pulpit* (March, 1968), p. 14.

[5] Frederick C. Grant, *Christ's Victory and Ours* (New York: The Macmillan Company, 1950), pp. 63-65.

However, that is not the finish, not the end of the matter for us. Think of it this way: a bridge builder dreams of a bridge. Then he sets to work. The chasm is spanned first by a cord, then by a cable, and then by steel. At last a bridge is built. The builder stands back to admire his work. "It is finished," he says. But really, it has just begun. For now the bridge is to be used; now the people go back and forth upon it. So Jesus said, "It is finished." But really it was just begun. The means were now available. The way was then open. But it remains for us to trust that unmerited, undeserved love of God, to step out on it, and trust that it will hold us up. Thus, using the bridge God himself has finished, we shall cross the chasm between us and him and we shall be the redeemed. Then, we shall be finished, too.

"Father, into your hands. . . ."

14. A Mother at Peace

Scripture: Luke 23:44-46

INTRODUCTION

The crucifixion was unrelieved tragedy for one person present—Mary, the mother of Jesus. We know she was there. The Gospels tell us she was standing near. Her presence at the foot of the cross was a triumph for motherly love. Nothing else brought her there. She does not seem to have been a believer or follower, at least not at that time. The New Testament record simply does not permit us to count her as one who had great faith in her son or his claims. She was not there as a faithful follower or steadfast believer. She was there as a loving mother, bewildered by all that had taken place.

Frankly, her relationship to Jesus is an enigma to us. According to the New Testament, Mary knew from the beginning that this child of hers was special and unique. The Gospels leave little doubt that she was supposed to have known this babe she brought forth was in fact the Christ. Yet subsequently she seemed not to know, or she seemed to have forgotten, or something like that. There is ample evidence to indicate that all was not well between Jesus and his family or between Jesus and his mother. Mary did not understand this son of hers. Yet she was there.

Let me offer a theory. Mary did know this child was someone very special. She knew he was destined for great things, but he himself seemed not to know. He seemed to do everything wrong.

119

He started by getting his own townspeople so angry with him they wanted to throw him off a cliff. He antagonized the important people and associated with the unimportant. He broke the sabbath laws. One time he made a shambles of the temple. She knew he was destined for great things, but he didn't seem to know it. And now at last, here she was at the cross. Her son born under such promise was dying in such shame. The angel's promise at his birth was still unfulfilled. One couldn't even believe angels anymore! That's Mary—poor, bewildered mother standing near the cross.

INTERVIEW

PREACHER: Mary, I confess I'm somewhat embarrassed to talk with you about that day.

MARY: Embarrassed? Why?

PREACHER: Well, I know it must have been a horrible experience for you—one you'd just as soon forget.

MARY: Yes, it was horrible all right. But I could never forget it, and really, I don't mind anymore talking about it.

PREACHER: Actually you were taking chances being out there, weren't you?

MARY: Maybe so—sometimes at executions the families of criminals were bothered or abused. But he was my son and there was no other place for me to be.

PREACHER: Did you ever think of him as a "criminal"?

MARY: *Me?* Oh, no, no—never! I didn't always understand him, but he never did anything wrong or bad!

PREACHER: It seems strange for you, his mother, to admit that you didn't understand him.

MARY: I know it must—and I'm not proud of it. Yet I didn't understand him then and I don't know anyone who did.

PREACHER: You mean no one understood him?

MARY: That's certainly the way it seemed. If they had understood him, they wouldn't have done that to him.

PREACHER: Well, what was it that you didn't understand?

MARY: That's a long story, but from the day he was born I had strange feelings about him.

PREACHER: Strange feelings? What do you mean?

MARY: I thought he was destined to do great things—to be a great leader of our people or a great servant of God.

PREACHER: And you don't think he became that?

120

MARY: I do now—but I didn't then.

PREACHER: Can you explain that for me?

MARY: It's not very complicated. I loved Jesus as any mother loves a son. Yet he didn't seem at all like a great leader out there. All the temple authorities were against him. The crowds were laughing at him; the soldiers spitting on him.

PREACHER: That wasn't a very pleasant scene.

MARY: No, and I stood there thinking about all those dreams I'd had—all those expectations that he might even be the Messiah. He didn't look like the Messiah that day!

PREACHER: Mary, you keep emphasizing what you felt and thought that day. I take it that you changed your mind about things later.

MARY: Oh, yes, I did. I understand him now. I know he was the Messiah, but not the Messiah most of us were looking for.

PREACHER: What made the difference? What changed your mind?

MARY: Mainly the resurrection and what happened after that.

PREACHER: How did all that change your mind?

MARY: Well, it seemed to prove that he was right and the rest of us were wrong.

PREACHER: Right about what?

MARY : Everything, really, but I suppose mainly about God.

PREACHER: And the resurrection proved that for you.

MARY: Yes, but I began to feel that way toward the end of the crucifixion.

PREACHER: Could you tell me about it?

MARY: Just before he died, Jesus said something that I suppose meant more to me than to anyone else.

PREACHER: What was that?

MARY: When he was a boy, I taught him a bedtime prayer. It was taken from one of our old Hebrew psalms. Each night when I tucked him into bed, he said that prayer and then went off to sleep.

PREACHER: Could you tell us what that prayer was?

MARY: Yes, it was: "Father, into thy hands I commit my spirit."

INTERPRETATION

A mother hears things others miss. We are glad Mary was there to hear all the comfort and hope in those last words of her son Jesus. Of course, those words had special meaning for her, and they can have special meaning for us. We, too, can hear comfort and hope in them. Actually they provide a victorious note in the midst of the horror of the crucifixion. Generally we reserve words like victory and triumph for Easter. Yet they are not inappropriate here in considering this seventh and final word from the cross. Easter declares a victory *over* death. The cross declares an equally significant victory *in* death.

Easter was a great victory celebration. Jesus won a victory over death. However, that great victory over death was possible only because of this other victory—the victory of the cross. Before the victory over death, there was the victory in death. The empty tomb would have been empty of meaning had it not been for the cross. It was the victory in death that made Easter believable. That is why we look so closely at the cross and listen so intently to its words. It is not because we enjoy the gruesome sight—God forbid. It's because we want to understand the full scope of the victory won there. Jesus took a method of criminal execution and transformed it into an instrument of redemption. He took a tool for life's destruction and transformed it into a means for life's salvation. He took that which always had stood for hate and transformed it so that it always shall stand for love. That is the greatness of his victory! The way in which he died was victory in itself. That victory in death reached its climax with the seventh and final word from the cross; the word Mary cherished above all others. "Father, into thy hands I commit my spirit." Resurrection was no surprise for one who died like that. Victory over death was to be expected for one who had won such a victory in death.

NO LEAP IN THE DARK

That seventh word means that for Jesus death was not a leap into the dark. Let me explain that! Jesus did not surrender his spirit to a great mystery. He committed himself to a great Father. Death to Jesus was not a fearful venture into a great, dark unknown. Others may think of it as that. To them, death is the inexplainable mystery. No one on earth has been to this mysterious region and returned. No human has the voice of experience in this matter. When we undergo anything else, a fellow human can comfort us saying, "I know—I've been through it." But not death—it is the great unknown. "The secret of heaven," said Emerson, "is kept from age to age."[1] No sociable, gossipy angel has dropped a hint. It

122

remains the world's best-kept secret. Reinhold Neibuhr, esteemed American theologian, put it this way: "We cannot describe either the furniture of heaven or the temperature of hell." So, death is the great unknown. It opens out on great mystery. We can understand what prompted one skeptic to say: "I am going to take a leap in the dark. I commit my body to the worms and my spirit to the Great Perhaps."[2]

However, for Jesus it was not a leap in the dark. He did not commit his spirit to a great perhaps, but to a great Father. Death may have been an unknown, but the Father was known. Jesus did not make a leap into the dark but a leap toward God. He did not draw near to a great mystery. He drew near instead to a great deity. He did not peer into a befogged and befuddled future. He looked instead to a beloved and beneficent Father. Mary told us how Jesus happened to know these words. They are found in Psalm 31. The fifth verse of that psalm has this phrase: "Into thy hand I commit my spirit." It was a psalm that Hebrew mothers taught their children, a psalm frequently used as a bedtime prayer in much the same way in which children today say, "Now I lay me down to sleep." However, Jesus made one significant addition to this ancient Hebrew prayer. He added the word "Father." The last words of a little Hebrew boy before sleep became the last words of this strong son of Abraham before death.[3] "Father, into thy hands I commit my spirit." John's Gospel says that when Jesus died, he "bowed his head" (John 19:30b). One scholar says that that is the exact language one would use to describe putting the head back on the pillow.[4] That's no leap in the dark.

Death may be an unknown, but the Father is known. We may not be able to describe the furniture of heaven or the temperature of hell. We may not have charts and maps of the afterlife, but we do have a Father. We have a Father into whose care we can commit ourselves. For us, too, death need not be a leap in the dark but a leap

[1] Harry Emerson Fosdick, ed.,*Rufus Jones Speaks to Our Time* (New York: The Macmillan Company, 1951), p. 279.

[2] A. Leonard Griffith, *Beneath the Cross of Jesus* (London: Lutterworth Press, 1962), p. 50.

[3] William Barclay, *The Gospel of Luke* (Philadelphia: The Westminster Press, 1956), p. 301.

[4] William Barclay, *The Gospel of John*, vol. 2 (Philadelphia: The Westminster Press, 1956), p. 301.

toward God. His parting prayer can be yours and mine: "Father, into thy hands I commit my spirit." For him and for us that's no leap in the dark.

NO THIEF IN THE NIGHT

Further, that seventh word means that for Jesus death was not a thief in the night. Let me explain that. Mary was impressed with the calmness of Jesus in the face of death. At least that's the way we interpreted her reactions. He died as calmly and peacefully as if he were going to sleep. There was nothing frantic about him. As a matter of fact, there was nothing frantic about him throughout all the last days of his life. That's one of the most impressive things about him. There was something frantic about his enemies. In a frenzy they manipulated the mob and planned the execution. There was something frantic about Pilate. Nervously he tried to wash away the guilt from his hands. But there never was anything frantic about Jesus. Throughout the whole tragic sequence of events Jesus never lost his control. He saw what was coming, but he did not panic. He knew disaster was on the way, but he didn't allow it to destroy him. He faced death, but he did not fear it. In short, death was not some thief in the night, stealing away his resources. Death was another event he faced with the same resources of faith and trust.

In war there is something called a sneak attack. When they least expect it, the enemies are assaulted. Surprised, caught unawares, there is little time to regroup. With no time to work out a new strategy, no time to throw up new defenses, no time for staff conferences on tactics, the enemy capitulates. Death was no sneak attack on Jesus. It did not take him by surprise, unawares, unprepared. The same resources that had been his in his living were his in his dying. He faced death on the same familiar ground of faith and trust. Those things which had been his strength in living were his strength in dying. Jesus lived as he died and died as he lived. His life had been committed to God—so, too, was his death.

It has been said that Jesus said nothing new in this seventh word. By committing his spirit into God's keeping, he was not sounding a new note.[5] His spirit always had been committed to God's

[5] Frederick C. Grant, *Christ's Victory and Ours* (New York: The Macmillan Company, 1950), p. 72.

124

keeping. All his life he had served the Father's will. It was to be expected that in death he would know the Father's presence. All his days he had sought to do the Father's will. It was to be expected that in death he would commit himself into that Father's hands. "Generally," said one preacher, "we die as we live. So it was with Jesus."[6] He lived with his spirit in God's care, and he died with his spirit in God's care. Generally a man dies as he lives. For Jesus, death was no thief in the night, stealing away his faith and trust. His resources in living were his resources in dying.

Rufus Jones told a story that is a favorite of mine. A little girl was riding on a train, seated next to a certain gentleman. Soon she and the man were friends, talking as though they had known each other forever. The man said, "In another hour you'll be at your city and get off the train." The girl replied, "I wish we would never reach that old city. I hate to get there." The man discovered that she and her mother were riding this train to a new home. The little girl had overheard her mother say to a friend that it was too bad her little girl had to leave the school where she had just learned the alphabet and start all over again in a new school. The girl had taken that to mean that all her hard work had been wasted and that in the new school she would have to learn an entirely new alphabet. The girl was comforted when the man explained that in the new city the same alphabet would be in use.[7] Fortunate is the man who on death does not have to learn a whole new alphabet. Fortunate is the man who all his life has been committed to God's will and keeping. Such a man faces death as he faced life on the firm ground of faith and trust. To such a one, death is not a thief in the dark stealing away his resources. It is another event to be faced with the same resources.

For Jesus, death was not a leap in the dark or a thief in the night. "Father"—nothing fearful or frantic about that. "Father, into thy hands I commit my spirit." Anyone who dies with a prayer like that will surely greet a resurrection morn.

[6] Clovis G. Chappell, *The Seven Words* (Nashville: Abingdon Press, 1952), p. 69.
[7] Harry Emerson Fosdick, ed., *Rufus Jones Speaks to Our Time* (New York: The Macmillan Company, 1951), p. 284.